To Vale

Enjoy!

Naomi
Wants to Know

from Naomi

Naomi
Wants to Know

Letters from a Little Girl to the Big Big World

Naomi Shavin

Fairview Press
Minneapolis

Published by Fairview Press, 2450 Riverside Avenue South, Minneapolis, MN 55454.

Library of Congress Cataloging-in-Publication Data
Shavin, Naomi, 1991–
    Naomi wants to know: letters from a little girl to the big big world/
    Naomi Shavin. -- 1st ed.
      p.   cm.
    ISBN 1-57749-076-2 (alk. paper)
    1. Shavin, Naomi, 1991–   --Correspondence. 2. Children--United
    States--Correspondence. 3. Children's writings, American. I. Title.
    CT275.S4523A4   1998
    973.929'092--dc21   98-35613
                                                                CIP

FIRST EDITION
First Printing: September 1998

Printed in the United States of America

02   01   00   99   98   7   6   5   4   3   2   1

Cover design: Laurie Duren
Book design and layout: Jessica Thoreson

Publisher's note: The publications of Fairview Press, including *Naomi Wants to Know*, do not necessarily reflect the philosophy of Fairview Health Services.

For a free catalog, call toll free 1–800–544–8207.

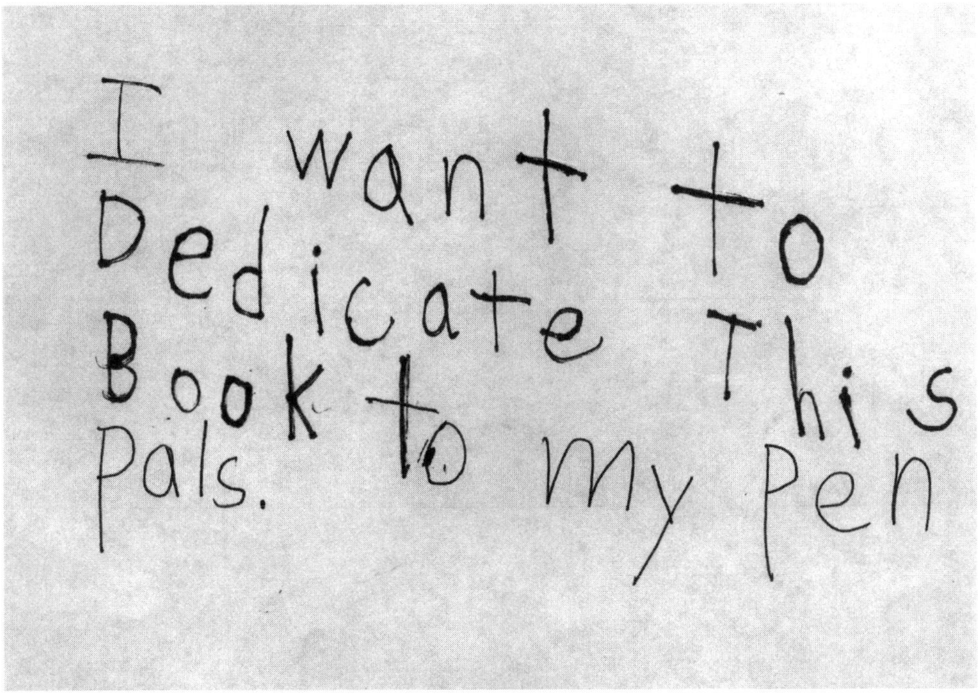

I want to
Dedicate This
Book to my Pen
Pals.

Contents

The Letters

Preface

The reason why I wrote this book is because It's like a prescription to other Children. I helps children learn to write and draw. I hope It encourages Parents to write It letters With their Children. Love Naomi

The reason why I wrote this book is because it is like
a prescription to other children. It helps children
learn to write and draw. I hope it encourages parents
to write letters with their children.

Love,

Naomi

Introduction

by Mark Shavin (Naomi's dad)

MY DAUGHTER, NAOMI, HAS A LOT OF QUESTIONS. Her mother and I cannot remember a time when she was not talking, singing, or asserting her strong opinions; but her letters to world leaders and corporate bigwigs, scientists, astronauts, God, and the Tooth Fairy are a relatively new phenomenon.

This book began with a single question. Naomi, five years old and a kindergarten student at a Jewish day school, wanted to know why Santa Claus was on the Coke cans. It was December, the month of Christmas and Hanukah, and she felt left out. I encouraged her to write a letter to the Coca-Cola Company. That first letter and the thoughtful, if ambiguous, reply led to more letters—to Queen Elizabeth, President Clinton, Coretta Scott King, and others. Naomi hasn't always gotten personal responses, but she has been excited, nevertheless, to get a letter from Buckingham Palace on a Friday and a letter from the White House the following Saturday. Truly, the world is her pen pal, and I am proud of her.

When Naomi turned four, we began keeping a journal together. That, I suppose, was the real precursor to the letters. The journal, which I wrote and she illustrated, became a daily record of her dreams and prayers, her feelings about her teachers, friends, and parents. Of my wife's father, remarkably fit and in his nineties, she remarked:

"Papa is old. I didn't know him when he was new."

The journal became a place to write of snowflakes and lightning bugs, honeysuckle and hot chocolate, even New Year's Resolutions. One was about my mother and my late father:

"I'm going to give Grandma Phyllis something to remind her of Grandpa Norman because I think she's terribly sad. I'm going to give her an old man."

We wanted to keep the journal honest so there's also room to remember the occasional temper tantrum:

"Yesterday was a bad, bad day because I was crying. There were all these things I was mad about that I kept screaming about."

The journal reminds me that, when I asked Naomi what God looked like, she replied:

"He has a round head. And he has feet and a long shirt and he has pants and he looks at us from up there with Mother Nature."

Naomi's observations would be lost to time and memory were they never recorded. Riding in the car, Naomi told her mother,

"Aren't you glad you don't live inside your body?"
"Why?" her mother asked.
"Because it stinks in there. Just smell your breath!"

One morning, exasperated because I was running late for work and couldn't find a pair of matching socks, I stomped downstairs where Naomi, her little brother Adam, and her mother were having breakfast.

"Look at this!" I demanded indignantly. *"I have five socks and no matches for any of them. Is this some kind of conspiracy?"*
My wife was filling out a form for Naomi's school and stopped to help me. *"Do you have any hobbies you want to share with Naomi's class?"* she asked, handing me the elusive socks.
"Hobbies?" I was incredulous. *"Who has time for hobbies? You mean, like bring something to school?"*
"Daddy," Naomi piped up, *"maybe you could bring in one of your socks!"*

The fact is I do have a hobby now, one that I share with Naomi. We write letters together. That first journal has evolved into a second one that is crammed with letters Naomi has penned to the National Hurricane Center, the National Labor Relations Board, Madeleine Albright, Princess Diana, the Reverend Howard Finster, and people who study tadpoles, earthquakes, earthworms and comets. In the process, we have both learned a lot about all kinds of things. How else would we have known that some worms leave behind a shiny-looking slime that helps them find their way home? How else would we have known there are six different lists of hurricane names, one used each year? How else would we have met Irece, a precious little girl at a local homeless shelter, whose lovely letter to Naomi brought us down to the shelter as volunteers?

There are innumerable benefits to writing letters with your child, but you should know at the outset that it requires patience. It's not easy coaxing a five- or six-year-old to write a letter to the Supreme Court of the United States. It's hard enough just getting her to eat spinach. The easiest letters are those that grow naturally out of conversation. The best ones are those that reflect the child's innate curiosity and innocence. Naomi's letter to the high court began with a question asked in the car: "What's jail like?"

There is no perfect time to compose a letter with a child who is just beginning to read and write, but, if you make the time, it will sharpen those skills. Sometimes Naomi and I write at the kitchen table on a lazy weekend afternoon. Other times she takes up the pen in her bedroom just before bedtime. Sometimes she does it on her own, but other times I have to prod her. I try to avoid putting thoughts in her head, but we spend a lot of time talking about the way the world works. By the way, Naomi always illustrates her letters, and this is her favorite part—the payoff for sandwiching a few perfect lines of prose between "Dear" and "Love, Naomi."

In case you're wondering, Naomi and I don't go in for this newfangled e-mail. We'd certainly save money on postage, but sometimes when you use the U.S. mail you get big packages and really nifty things in return, and we like that a lot. I have found the Internet to be an invaluable tool in finding addresses. When Naomi wanted to write to "the eskimoes," I used the Internet to find a school a few hundred miles from the Arctic Circle. Weeks later an entire kindergarten class drew pictures for Naomi, illustrating life in the tiny village of Point Lay, Alaska.

When sending out Naomi's correspondence, I have found it useful to supply a cover letter to clarify her handwriting. Her handwriting can resemble the tremors of a seismograph. I also provide a return address. I always explain that I helped Naomi with her spelling, but the sentiments are her own. I also make copies of the letters to put in her journal—a lasting record of her state of mind at ages five and six.

This brings me to the great benefit of writing with your child, whether in a journal or in letter form. It is an opportunity to capture your child's voice before it is lost to the cacophony of adult thought. No doubt you take pictures and videotapes of your child. Consider jotting down your child's ideas and wishes and unintentional one-liners. They don't have to vanish like shooting stars, lost to the dimming years. If you write letters, keep copies, tuck them into your child's journal. Save them today and you will savor them tomorrow.

One more thing. Buy a roll of stamps.

Naomi and her dad, Mark Shavin

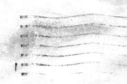

The Letters

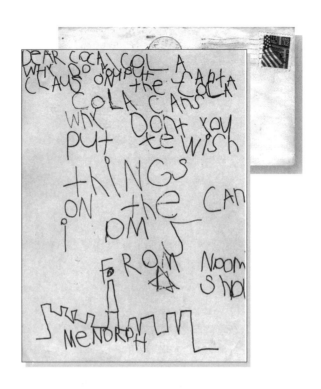

Dear Coca-Cola,

    Why do you put Santa Claus on the Coca-Cola cans?

    Why don't you put Jewish things on the cans?

    I am 5.

From Naomi Shavin

Naomi's letter to the Coca-Cola Company was her very first one. I could have written to the company myself, but it was her question, not mine, and it carried more weight coming from a five-year-old.

The Coca-Cola Company

COCA-COLA PLAZA
ATLANTA, GEORGIA

ADDRESS REPLY TO
P. O. DRAWER 1734
ATLANTA, GA 30301

1-800-438-2653

January 8, 1997

Ms. Naomi Shavin
980 Edgewater Dr., N.W.
Atlanta, GA 30328

Dear Naomi:

Roberto Goizueta asked me to thank you for your thoughtful letter. We
are happy to respond to your question about our holiday packaging.

Naomi, the goal of our advertising has always been to appeal to as
many people in our large target market as possible. It is our hope
that the current holiday packaging for Coca-Cola featuring the
Sundblom Santa does just that.

Haddon Sundblom first created his famous Santa in 1931 as advertising
for Coca-Cola. We think this Santa has universal appeal. We have
used his cheerful image of peace and goodwill year after year!

We want you to know, Naomi, that The Coca-Cola Company understands our
culture is made up of many different types of people. We try with our
holiday packaging to help our consumers remember times of social and
family associations rather than religious ones.

We thank you for writing with your great question, Naomi. I hope you
will enjoy the enclosed items.

Sincerely,

Susan Righter
Susan Righter
Consumer Affairs Specialist

Encl: Refreshing Facts
       Ruler
       Sticker Postcard

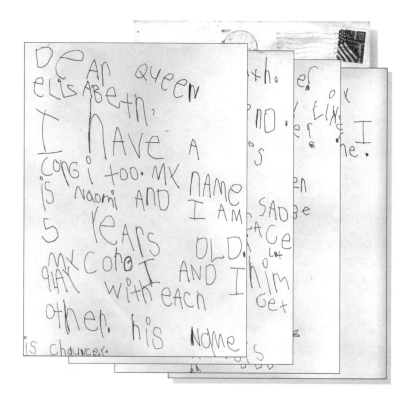

Dear Queen Elizabeth,

I have a corgi, too. My name is Naomi and I am 5 years old. My corgi and I play with each other. His name is Chauncey. He has stinky breath. He is my best friend.

He spends his day sleeping. He always has a sad look on his face. No one spends a lot of time with him and he doesn't get much love. What are your corgis and children like? What do they all look like? How do you rule all those people? If I were Queen my rule would be no being mean!

Love, Naomi

P.S. I named my pet turtle after you because I like your name.

Naomi was intrigued to learn she had something in common with the Queen of England. The Queen rules Great Britain. Naomi rules a world of insects and amphibians. Both answer to their dogs: Welsh corgis.

BUCKINGHAM PALACE

24th February 1997

Dear Naomi,

I am commanded by The Queen to write and thank you for your letter.

Her Majesty thought it was kind of you to write to her but as The Queen receives many letters each day, I am afraid it is not possible for her to reply to them personally.

I am, however, enclosing some information which you may like to have and I am to thank you again for your letter.

Yours sincerely

Lady-in-Waiting

BUCKINGHAM PALACE FACT SHEET

ROYAL DOGS

CORGIS

King George VI, while Duke of York, purchased the first Royal corgi in 1933, after admiring a friend's dog. *Dookie* came from the Rozavel Kennels in Surrey and was a Pembrokeshire corgi. In 1936, The King acquired a second corgi called *Jane*, who had a litter on Christmas Eve. Two of these puppies were kept. They were named *Crackers* and *Carol*.

The Queen as a child therefore grew up with these dogs and for her eighteenth birthday she was given *Susan*, a bitch from a Cambridgeshire kennel who was born on 20th February, 1944, and died aged fourteen on 26th January, 1959, at Sandringham. *Sugar* and *Heather* also have gravestones there, as The Queen's dogs are usually buried in the grounds of the house in which Her Majesty is living at that time.

The Queen bred from *Susan* and now has corgis of the tenth generation, directly descended from her first dog. *Pipkin* a dachshund belonging to Princess Margaret, was also mated with a corgi bitch and the resulting offspring are known as 'dorgis'.

Her Majesty looks after her own dogs as much as possible. They live in her private apartments and often travel with The Queen within the United Kingdom.

LABRADORS AT SANDRINGHAM KENNELS

Queen Alexandra possessed many breeds of dogs, including the Sandringham strain of black labradors founded in 1911. After her death in 1925, King George V changed the Royal prefix at the Kennel Club from Wolferton to Sandringham. He also re-introduced the Clumber breed of spaniels, favoured for their rough-shooting ability.

During the short reign of King Edward VIII (Duke of Windsor), the kennels were closed and there were no dogs at Sandringham.

When King George VI came to the Throne in 1936, he re-established the kennels with yellow labradors, which he used only as shooting dogs. In 1949, it was decided that the famous labrador dog, *Windsor Bob*, should be brought to Sandringham for breeding purposes. Because of the great interest taken by The Queen, the breeding programme has gone from strength to strength.

The kennels are situated on the southern boundary of the grounds of Sandringham House. They surround The Kennels House, which is occupied by The Queen's Head Keeper and Dog Handler. There are usually about twenty fully grown dogs at Sandringham, from the older and more experienced gundogs used by members of the Royal Family during the shooting season to the younger dogs undergoing training. In addition to provided dogs for the Royal Family, the Estate Gamekeepers are kept supplied with working labradors and spaniels. At certain times of the year, usually in the spring and early summer, one or two of the best bitches are used for breeding and there may be a dozen or so puppies in the kennels as well.

It is the aim of the Sandringham kennels to attain the highest standards possible and to achieve this, a great deal of time is spent training the best dogs up to Field Trial level. In recent years, there have been five Field Trial Champions, namely *Sandringham Ranger, Sandringham Slipper, Sherry of Biteabout, Sandringham Salt* and *Sandringham Sydney*. The latter because became particularly well-known because of a television film made in 1977, entitled 'Sandringham Sydney & Co.'.

Although Sandringham House and Grounds are open to visitors during the summer months, the kennels are NOT open to the public.

****

THE QUEEN'S CORGIS AND DORGIS

CORGIS	DORGIS
Phoenix	*Harris*
Pharos	*Brandy*
Kelpie	*Cider*
Swift	*Berry*

January, 1997.

When Fairview Press decided to publish Naomi's letters, there was one stipulation: that we seek releases from her pen pals. A few of the releases, like this one from Buckingham Palace, were as interesting as the initial correspondence.

BUCKINGHAM PALACE

23rd February, 1998

Dear Mr Shavin,

     Thank you for your recent letter. We have no objection to Fairview Press publishing, in the planned collection of letters entitled "Naomi Wants To Know", the letter from the Lady-in-Waiting that your daughter Naomi received last year. Please accept this letter as confirmation of that position.

     Since Naomi wrote I am sorry to say that one of The Queen's corgis, Phoenix, has sadly died. However Naomi will, I am sure, be glad to hear that Her Majesty has a new corgi, Emma, to take the place of Phoenix.

Yours sincerely,

David Tuck
Assistant Press Secretary to The Queen

Mr Mark Shavin

Naomi and her corgi, Chauncey

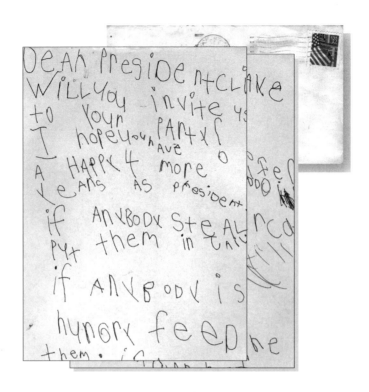

Dear President Clinton,

Will you invite us to your party? I hope you have a happy 4 more years as President.

If anybody steals, put them in jail. If anybody is hungry, feed them. If anybody is sick, make sure they eat apples.

Love, Naomi

P.S. How is your wife? How is your child doing? How is your cat?

I told Naomi about President Clinton's re-election, about his upcoming inauguration, about the M&Ms on Air Force One. We talked about the duties and the power of a president, and she felt it important to offer some advice.

Thank you for writing to me. I always enjoy hearing from young people. You are the future of our country, and I am honored to be your President.

PRESIDENT BILL CLINTON
42nd President of the United States

Inauguration:	January 20, 1993
Vice President:	Al Gore
Wife:	Hillary Rodham Clinton
Daughter:	Chelsea Clinton
Born:	August 19, 1946 in Hope, Arkansas
Education:	Georgetown University, Bachelor of Science Degree 1968
	Oxford University, Rhodes Scholar 1968-70
	Yale Law School, Law Degree 1973
Career:	Assistant Professor of Law, University of Arkansas School of Law 1973-76
	Arkansas Attorney General 1977-79
	Arkansas Governor 1979-81; 1983-92

Dear Mrs. King,

   I'm sorry your husband died. How are your children doing? I'm learning about your husband in school. They taught us that he was a great American. He helped the black people. He changed the laws. It made the black people feel better, but the white people are still kind of mean. I know the golden rule. Treat others the way you would like to be treated.

   The person who is writing you is Naomi. Do you know Rosa Parks? She was black and did not give up her seat. Whoever gets there first should get the seat.

Love,

Naomi

Every year at the Epstein School, the children learn about Martin Luther King, Jr. During a visit to her kindergarten class, I was astonished at how much they already knew, and was touched, particularly when they broke into a spontaneous rendition of "We Shall Overcome."

THE KING CENTER

February 3, 1997

Ms. Naomi Shavin
980 Edgewater Dr., N.W.
Atlanta, Georgia 30328

Dear Naomi,

I was so glad to learn that you are studying about the life and work of my husband, Martin Luther King, Jr., and I write to encourage you to learn about his teachings and the things he did for our country and world.

Martin Luther King, Jr.'s message of love for people of all races is more important than ever as we work together to create a better nation and world. I hope you will help carry on his work by being nonviolent toward all people.

My husband believed that all children are special because God created everyone, and that everybody has something great to give to the world. He would want me to urge you to study hard, because education is the key to having a good life and making a more just and caring world for all people.

I hope you will have a great year in school and that you and all of your schoolmates will help each other like brothers and sisters. I wish you the best and I look forward to hearing of your achievements in the future.

Sincerely,

Coretta Scott King

Coretta Scott King

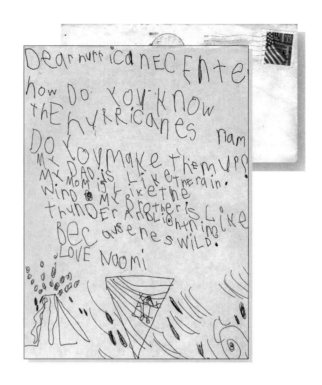

Dear Hurricane Center,

How do you know the hurricanes' names?

Do you make them up?

My dad is like the rain. My mom is like the wind. My brother is like thunder and lightning because he's wild.

Love,

Naomi

Naomi was learning about hurricanes in school. I sent her to class with a front page article about Hurricane Erin. Later we read "The Magic School Bus Visits a Hurricane." That answered a lot of her questions but not all of them. She didn't realize, for instance, that hurricanes are named as they form, believing instead that they've always had their names, and it's up to the rest of us to figure out who they are.

U.S. DEPARTMENT OF COMMERCE
National Oceanic and Atmospheric Administration

Tropical Prediction Center
National Hurricane Center
11691 S.W. 17th Street
Miami, FL 33165-2149

January 30, 1997

Naomi Shavin
980 Edgewater Drive N.W.
Atlanta, Georgia 30328

Dear Naomi:

We enjoyed your letter very much, and we share your interest in hurricanes. Most of our forecasters were also facinated with hurricanes as children.

As to the Hurricane names, we have six lists of names. We use one list each year. The first name on the list starts with the letter "A", the second name starts with "B", and so on. Girl's names are followed by boy's names, and we try to use names from all of the countries in this part of the world. You will hear many familiar sounding names (including Bible names like yours), and some that are unfamiliar. Most of those are Spanish language names. The names were selected anout 20 years ago, and are only changed when a hurricane is so terrible that it alone should be remembered by that name. Andrew, which occurred about the time you were born, has been retired. That place on the list is now given to Alex.

If you, and your very interesting family, are ever in southern Florida, it would be my pleasure to show you around the National Hurricane Center. Keep up the interest in hurricanes, work hard in school, and you have my best wishes for the future.

Sincerely,

Jerry D. Jarrell
Deputy Director

15

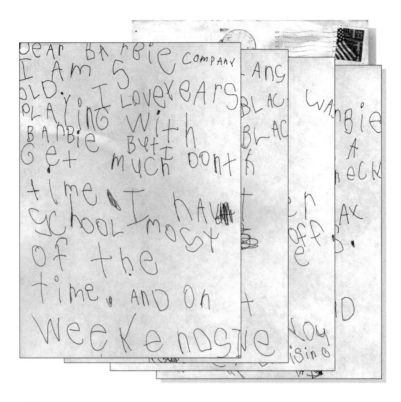

Dear Barbie Company,

I am 5 years old. I love playing with Barbie, but I don't get much time. I have school most of the time and on weekends I already have plans.

I have black eyes. I have blackish-brown hair with highlights. Why don't the Barbie's heads tilt back? Mine broke. One night I was playing with my Whitney Barbie and her head fell off. Will you give me a new one? Why don't you make exercising things for Barbie? My brother is a pain in the neck. He never lets me play Barbies.

Your friend,

Naomi

Naomi's world revolves around a lethargic corgi, kindergarten, and Barbie. When her mother and I are not driving her to school, working, or mediating disputes between her and her brother, we are trying to keep track of Barbie's shoes. In my daughter's pint-sized universe, Barbie has more shoes than her mother and Imelda Marcos combined. How preoccupied is she with Barbie? Her journal reminds me that one night, as I was putting Naomi to bed, she said, "Daddy, sometimes when I go to sleep I hear my Barbies talking."

"Does that scare you?" I asked.

"No," she replied, "but sometimes I hear my Barbies getting dressed. That scares me!"

Naomi got a prompt response from Jill Barad, the President and CEO of Mattel, along with a second letter from Mattel's Worldwide Director of Consumer Affairs, who sent Naomi a "Pretty Hearts" Barbie. However, Mattel asked that we not reprint their letters, and we have honored that request. Suffice it to say that Ms. Barad noted Naomi's lament that she doesn't have enough time for her Barbie dolls and seemed to appreciate my five-year-old's very busy schedule.

Dear Homeless,

I want to give you a present. I'm giving it to you because you're poor and I wish you weren't. It makes me sad.

I'm sending a Barbie. I'd like to give you toys every weekend, but I don't have that many to spare.

Love,

Naomi

P.S. Can my family help make the dessert at the shelter?

Naomi sent the "Pretty Hearts" Barbie she received from Mattel.

THE ATLANTA UNION MISSION

165 ALEXANDER STREET, NW • P.O. BOX 1807 • ATLANTA, GA 30301
PHONE 404•588•4000   FAX 404•588•4016

Jill D. Mays, MS, MAC, LP
DIRECTOR OF WOMEN'S & CHILDREN'S SERVIC

April 23, 1997

Miss Naomi Shavin
Mr. Mark Shavin
980 Edgewater Drive N.W.
Atlanta, Georgia 30328

Dear Naomi,

I would like to sincerely thank you for your caring and generous spirit. The doll was given to a 5 year old little girl named Irece. She was delighted to receive it. Enclosed is a letter and a picture that Irece is sending to you. She wrote it herself, her mom helped her with the spelling. I hope you like it.

We would be delighted to have you and your family come help make dessert at the shelter. Please ask your dad to call Kelly Cramer the Volunteer Coordinator at 404-588-4009 ext.227 to set up a time to come in. I look forward to meeting you.

Sincerely yours,

Tracy Gibbs
Afterschool Coordinator

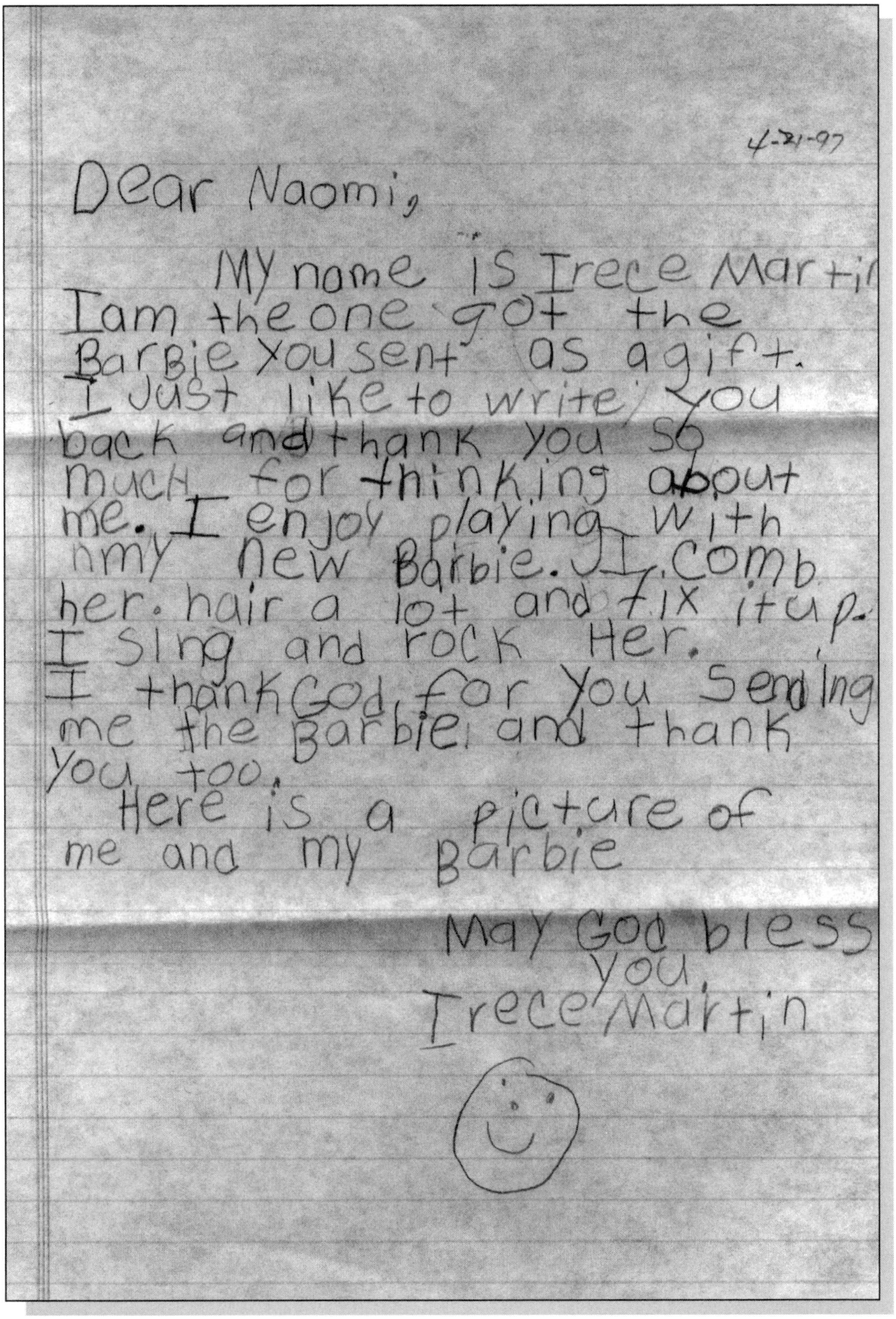

Dear Naomi,

My name is Irece Martin
I am the one got the
Barbie you sent as a gift.
I just like to write you
back and thank you so
much for thinking about
me. I enjoy playing with
my new Barbie. I comb
her hair a lot and fix it up.
I sing and rock her.
I thank God for you sending
me the Barbie and thank
you too.
Here is a picture of
me and my Barbie

May God bless
you,
Irece Martin

Me

Irece
5yrs.

Barbie
1yr.old

Naomi's mother cried at the letter from Irece. Naomi had to meet her. The following Saturday morning, Naomi and I drove down to "My Sister's House," a homeless shelter for women and children. I told Naomi we would help out, but there was no guarantee Irece would even be there.

We introduced ourselves to a staffer, and within five minutes I heard a woman's booming voice echo down a hallway. "Naomi is here? Where is that Naomi?" It was Irece's mother. She was delighted to see us. She told me that the Barbie doll had arrived on the very day Irece was fretting over the loss of another doll. I told her how touched we were by Irece's thank-you note. And, as we talked, the girls fell into an immediate and easy companionship as only children can. Irece's mother was lovely. She spoke a bit about her family, said they were not really homeless, but traveling from shelter to shelter, from state to state, ministering to those in need of spiritual guidance. After the girls played, Naomi and I helped prepare lunch. It was one of her first experiences with volunteerism.

Before leaving our house that morning, I happened to read in the Atlanta Journal-Constitution *Jimmy Carter's remarks at the Presidents' Summit for America's Future in Philadelphia. He noted that "most of us live a mundane or humdrum life with very little challenge or adventure or excitement or unpredictability about it.... It's an adventure in itself to reach out to someone who's different, who we don't even understand."*

I discussed these sentiments with Naomi as we made our way to the shelter, and we talked about them again on the way home. I encouraged her to write a letter about her experience, and she addressed it to America's foremost volunteer.

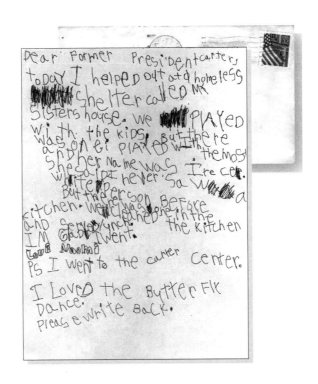

Dear Former President Carter,

    Today I helped out at a homeless shelter called My Sister's House. We played with the kids, but there was one I played with the most and her name was Irece. She said, "I never saw a white person before." But there was one in the kitchen. We cleaned the kitchen and served lunch. I'm glad I went.

Love,

Naomi

P.S. I went to the Carter Center. I loved the butterfly dance. Please write back.

**THE
CARTER
PRESIDENTIAL
CENTER**

6/4/97

To Naomi -
Thanks for your nice
note. I'm glad you
visited My Sister's House
and met Irece and
the other Children.
Love, and best wishes,

Jimmy Carter

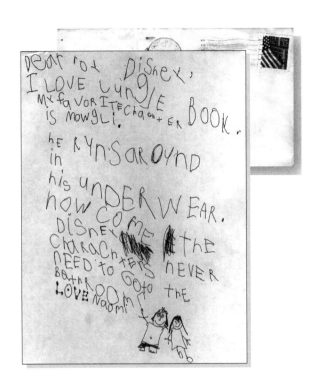

Dear Roy Disney,

    I love "Jungle Book." My favorite character is Mowgli. He runs around in his underwear. How come the Disney characters never need to go to the bathroom?

Love,

Naomi

My wife and I buy Naomi and her little brother every Disney movie out on video. We own Disney stock. And we're overrun by plastic action figures that delight our children but frequently send the vacuum cleaner to the shop for costly repairs. I suggested Naomi direct her letter and question to Roy Disney, hoping he might see in her drawing an early hint of a future animator.

The Walt Disney Company wrote back, but, like Mattel, did not want its response reprinted. This was somewhat perplexing because the letter was rather clever. In response to her question, "How come the Disney characters never need to go to the bathroom?" Naomi was informed that since she only sees them for a few hours out of their day, they've already gone to the bathroom, so they can spend their entire time on the big screen entertaining her. I asked Naomi what she thought of this reply. She thought it was ridiculous.

Dear Shannon,

What was it like in space? Was it dangerous? Could you touch Saturn with your hand? Have you ever made mistakes in space? When I look at the sky I think of my Grandpa Norman who died.

Love,

Naomi

Writing letters and sharing the newspaper are ways of teaching a child that the world is bigger than her backyard. I told Naomi about Shannon Lucid's 181 days aboard the Mir space station, that Shannon Lucid had spent more time living in space than any American or any woman. On the Internet we read about how Shannon Lucid knew she wanted to explore space from the time she was in fourth grade. I tell Naomi she can do and be whatever she wants. We talk about accomplishing goals and what that means and how that's done. Writing a letter is a way of setting a goal and accomplishing it. We got back form letters dispatched by the NASA publicity machine, but we enjoyed them just the same.

October 31, 1996

Dear Students,

Thank you so much for the great cards, booklets and letters.
It has been so enjoyable to read and look through all your
creations. I am glad that you are all so enthusiastic about
the space program.   I hope that someday you will be
welcoming back astronauts that have gone to Mars or coming
back from there yourself.

I had a great time on my mission on the Russian space station
Mir. And yes, since it was a Russian space station, we spoke
Russian the entire time that we were there. Most of my days
were spent working in the science module named Priroda. I
really enjoyed doing all the experiments, especially when it
involved growing plants.

The food was great. We had both Russian and American food.
But there were not very many deserts so sometimes I really
wanted some M&Ms. There is no shower on Mir so I had to wait
for that until I returned to earth. To keep my hair clean, I
just used a liquid shampoo that I put directly in my hair and
then rubbed it out with a towel. I never had to do laundry.
When I changed clothes, I just threw the used ones away.

I was able to talk to my family once a week on the radio and
I was also able to send and receive letters by e-mail. My
husband sent me a note every day. I thought that was really
great!!! I had a wonderful time during my six months in
space, but I was really glad to get back home to my family.

I hope that all you keep your strong interest in exploring
space and that some of you will be able to live and work in
space in the future!!

Sincerely,

Dear Grandpa Norman,

Someday I'll see you. We can get together. Even though I never knew you, I know you are inside me.

I love my dad.

I love you.

I hope the wind carries this to you.

Love,

Naomi

Naomi was born three years after my father died. She is named for him and is well aware that she has filled a void left by his absence. One night, snuggling in bed, she asked me, "Did I take your Dad's pal place?" In her journal, she dictated the following letter about him and about me: "Dear Grandpa Norman, I wish you would stay down for a long time so I could see you. I know what you look like because I have a picture of you. Your little boy's grown up now. He's very nice."

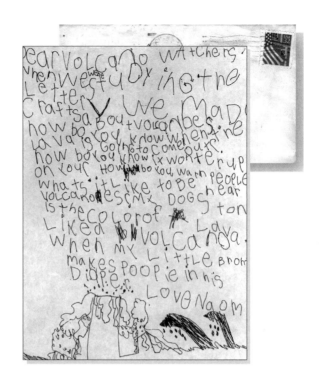

Dear Volcano Watchers,

When we were studying the letter "V," we made crafts about volcanoes. How do you know when the lava is going to come out? How do you know it won't erupt on you? How do you warn people? What's it like to be near volcanoes?

My dog's tongue is the color of lava. It's like a volcano when my little brother makes poopie in his diaper.

Love,

Naomi

No reply.

Dear Justice Ginsburg,

My grandmother has the name Ruth, too. I call her Ruru.

You are like King Solomon. You both decide stuff. He was the smartest king. One woman stole another woman's baby. King Solomon knew whose baby it was.

Are you in charge of all the people in the United States of America? Have you ever made a mistake?

Love,

5-Year-Old Naomi

May 8, 1997

Naomi Shavin
980 Edgewater Drive NW
Atlanta, GA 30328

Dear Naomi:

Thank you for your wonderful letter. Thinking about you,
your words, and your drawing, I have been smiling all day.

I have two grandchildren. My grandson is named Paul, and my
granddaughter is named Clara. Paul is 10 and Clara is 6. They
call me "Bubbie."

In answer to your questions, I am not in charge of all the
people in the United States, but I work hard to do my judging job
well. And yes, I have made many mistakes, but I try to learn
from them so that I will not make the same mistake twice.

Please tell your father I am glad he wrote to me, because I
did not receive your letter the first time it was mailed to me.

Keep up the good work you are doing in school.

Every good wish to you, your parents, and your grandmother,
Ruru,

Ruth Bader Ginsburg

Ruth Bader Ginsburg

One day Naomi and I were riding in the car and from the backseat she piped up, *"Daddy, what's jail like?" I am happy to say I had no personal knowledge, but the conversation that ensued led to a discussion of our court system, lawyers, guilt and innocence, and the work of judges. When discussing grownup topics, I try to relate them back to Naomi's world or find some other frame of reference. She had heard of King Solomon, so we talked about him.*

The first time Naomi sent her letter, she didn't hear anything. I wasn't sure at first if we should send it again. But I read Justice Ginsburg's comments about parenting and the judiciary in the book "Mothers and Daughters," and my wife Marla had the good fortune to meet the authors, Carol Saline and Sharon Wohlmuth. Marla told them about Naomi's correspondence, and they assured her that it was exactly the kind of letter Justice Ginsburg would warm to had she ever received it in the first place. So we sent it again. Not only did we get a warm reply, we got a cartoon with an inscription.

"That's right...five-ninths pepperoni and four-ninths sausage."

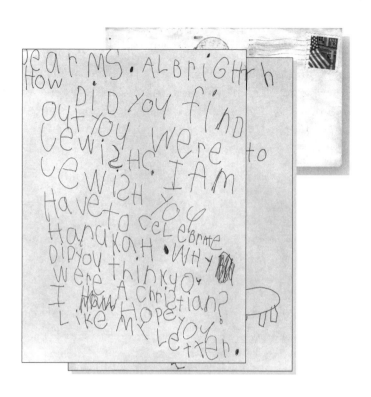

Dear Ms. Albright,

 How did you find out you were Jewish?

 I am Jewish. You have to celebrate Hanukah.

 Why did you think you were a Christian?

 I hope you like my letter.

 Be happy with who you are.

Love,

Naomi

P.S. Do you want to come to my house?

Children are often quietly tuned in to the world of adult conversation, which explains why we often find ourselves spelling words we're not ready to share. For instance, "Should we take the kids for i-c-e c-r-e-a-m?" Marla and I were in the upstairs hallway discussing news reports about Madeleine Albright belatedly finding out she had Jewish parents. "Can you believe she didn't know she was Jewish?" my wife asked aloud. Naomi wandered out of the bathroom. "Who didn't know she was Jewish?" I explained the role of the Secretary of State in terms she could understand—that the Secretary of State speaks to world leaders on behalf of the United States and, when there is trouble afoot, she gets on a plane and tries to put an end to it.

THE SECRETARY OF STATE
WASHINGTON

May 30, 1997

Dear Naomi:

I want to thank you for your letter concerning my Jewish heritage. I am enclosing for your interest some materials which I know your father will read to you which contain a lot of information about it.

It is heartening to know young people understand the importance of faith and community in this diverse and complicated world in which we live.

Thank you for the drawing of your house. I hope I get to meet you during one of my visits to Atlanta.

Sincerely,

Madeleine K. Albright

Miss Naomi Shavin,
    980 Edgewater Drive NW,
        Atlanta, GA.

Dear Tooth Fairy,

I was in the car eating a lolli when my tooth came out. Only a Barbie's head could fit in the space that my tooth left.

Please leave my tooth for one night. I want to show it to my friends. Today is a special day because it is Grandpa Norman's birthday and I lost my first tooth.

Love,

Naomi

Naomi's first letter to the Tooth Fairy was left beneath her pillow on March 2, 1997. It captures a momentous event in the life of a child in her own words.

From The Office of

THE TOOTH FAIRY

DEAR NAOMI,

I HAVE BEEN WAITING AND WAITING FOR THAT TOOTH TO FALL OUT. I THOUGHT IT WOULD FALL OUT WHEN YOU ATE AN APPLE. IT DID NOT. I THOUGHT IT WOULD FALL OUT WHEN YOU ATE CINNAMON TOAST. IT DID NOT. I THOUGHT IT WOULD FALL OUT WHEN YOU KEPT PUSHING IT BACK AND FORTH WITH YOUR FINGER.   IT DID NOT. SO IT'S ABOUT TIME.

THANK YOU FOR YOUR WONDERFUL LETTER, NAOMI. YOU ARE SO SMART. YOU CAN CERTAINLY KEEP YOUR TOOTH FOR ANOTHER DAY TO SHOW YOUR FRIENDS.   KEEP IT LONGER THAN THAT IF YOU WOULD LIKE TO SHOW IT TO YOUR GRANDPARENTS OR YOUR COUSINS OR ANY OTHER SPECIAL PEOPLE. PLEASE TAKE CARE OF ALL OF YOUR TEETH. BRUSH THEM IN THE MORNING AND AT NIGHT.

LOVE,

THE TOOTH FAIRY

P.S. BE NICE TO YOUR BROTHER

Dear Tooth Fairy,

I was playing with my tooth and I dropped it on the side of the car seat. I lost it.

Love,

Naomi

Written the day after her first letter.

From The Office of

THE TOOTH FAIRY

DEAR NAOMI,

HERE'S A POEM I WROTE FOR YOU. I HOPE YOU LIKE IT.

NAOMI'S TOOTH

WHEN I REACHED BENEATH YOUR PILLOW,
I THOUGHT I'D FIND YOUR TOOTH,
INSTEAD I FOUND A LETTER
IT TOLD THE BITTER TRUTH.

THE TOOTH THAT I'D BEEN PROMISED
WAS LOST ALONG THE WAY,
IT NEVER MADE IT TO MY HANDS,
DON'T WORRY I'LL STILL PAY.

THE MONEY THAT I LEFT BEHIND
IS YOURS TO SPEND OR KEEP,
IT'S YOURS FOR GIVING ME THE JOY
OF WATCHING WHILE YOU SLEEP.

YOUR CHESTNUT HAIR AGAINST THE SHEETS
YOUR PERFECT, HEART-SHAPED FACE,
YOUR TENDER ARMS, YOUR TINY HANDS
THEY'RE MADE TO BE EMBRACED.

I WONDER WHAT YOU DREAM TONIGHT
ARE YOU RUNNING THROUGH THE HILLS?
IS YOUR LITTLE BROTHER WITH YOU?
ARE YOU PICKING DAFFODILS?

I GUESS I'LL NEVER REALLY KNOW
FOR LIKE THE RIVER I MUST GO,
THE SUN IS RISING, GEESE ARE FLYING
AND NOW IT'S TIME FOR YOU TO GROW..

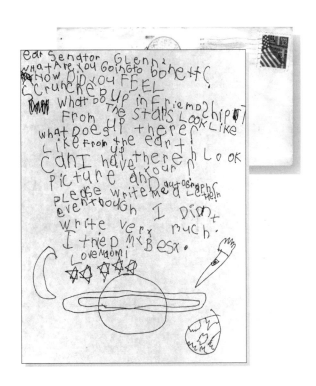

Dear Senator Glenn,

What are you going to do next?

How did you feel scrunched up in Friendship 7? What do the stars look like from up there? What does the earth look like from up there?

Can I have your picture and autograph? Please write me a letter even though I didn't write very much. I tried my best.

Love,

Naomi

Naomi and I were looking over the newspaper and there was an article about the 35th anniversary of John Glenn's historic space flight and his impending retirement from the U.S. Senate. "John Glenn," I explained, "was the original Buzz Lightyear."

To Naomi —
John Glenn

Dear Earthworm Scientist,

I know why earthworms have a head. They eat the ground and make doody. It's good for the plants.

Do earthworms have eyes? How do they see?

I have 10 earthworms as a pet. How do they talk?

Love,

Earthworm-catcher Naomi

From astronomy to agronomy, Naomi has a keen interest in the world above her head and beneath her feet. Naomi is a doting parent to earthworms and any other crawling thing she can fit in a pickle jar. Sometimes writing the letter is easier than finding someone to send it to, but the Internet is an invaluable tool for solving that problem. I was lucky enough to find Eileen J. Kladivko while trying to broaden Naomi's wormy horizons.

PURDUE UNIVERSITY

DEPARTMENT OF AGRONOMY
CROP, SOIL & ENVIRONMENTAL SCIENCES

April 2, 1997

Naomi Shavin
980 Edgewater Dr. NW
Atlanta, Georgia   30328

Dear Naomi,

Thank you very much for the letter you sent me on March 11. I am glad to hear you are an "earthworm catcher" and that you have 10 earthworms as pets. We also go and catch earthworms during our scientific studies. We like to know how many earthworms live in different kinds of soils that are growing different kinds of plants. We do this so we can help farmers who like to have more earthworms in their fields.

You asked whether earthworms have eyes, and how do they see. No, earthworms do not have eyes. This is because they live in the ground most of the time, where it's dark, so it would be hard to see even if they did have eyes. Although they don't actually see, they are sensitive to light. You know how sometimes if you lift up some leaves and there were earthworms underneath, they'll move quickly and try to get covered up again? One reason they do this is that the sunlight can hurt them, and they can "sense" the light even though they can't see. So they try to get out of the light.

Earthworms don't talk to each other, but they can communicate by touch and smell. Earthworms can know where other earthworms have been recently, by the feel and smell of the "slime" that they leave in their holes. Have you seen the shiny-looking slime that covers the worms and is sometimes in their holes? This helps the soil but also lets other worms know they've been there. For some worms it even helps them find their way home!

Thanks for the drawing of you and your earthworm jar. I hope you continue to have fun with earthworms and learn more about them.

Sincerely,

Eileen J. Kladivko

Dear Dinosaur Scientist,

Will you invite me and my family to dig up fossils?

If my brother was a dinosaur he would be called Wild-saurus. He's wild.

My mom would be Nice-asaurus. She's nice to me.

Were alligators friendly with dinosaurs?

Love,

Naomi

No reply.

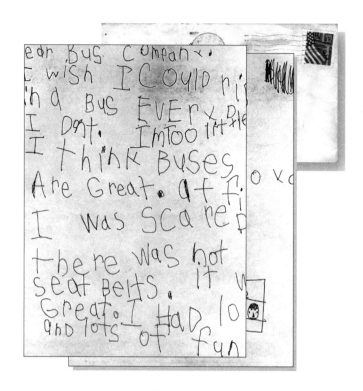

Dear Bus Company,

I wish I could ride in a bus every day. I don't. I'm too little. I think buses are great. At first I was scared. There was not seat belts. It was great. I had lots and lots of fun. I liked when it bumped up and down.

If there's an accident, how do you get the children out?

Love,

Naomi

Naomi rode her first school bus when her kindergarten class took a field trip to the Carter Presidential Center. That morning she woke up in tears. She was afraid because she knew the bus wouldn't have seat belts. Today's children are safety-conscious. They'll remind you in harsh tones if you forget to buckle them in. They grow up in car seats, then graduate to booster seats, and are often banished from the front seat entirely, particularly if there is a passenger-side airbag. Naomi's letter to the bus company was a way of allaying some of her fears.

TRANSIT, INC.

1014 VINE STREET, SUITE 1625, CINCINNATI, OHIO 45202, (513) 723-8700, FAX (513) 723-8704

March 25, 1997

Ms. Naomi Shavin
980 Edgewater Drive, NW
Atlanta, GA 30328

Dear Naomi:

I am pleased that you had a fun ride on the school bus. Please don't worry about the fact that there are no seat belts on your school bus, because it is designed to be safe without them. It is very important for you that when you are boarding and exiting the bus that you observe the rules of school bus safety. I have enclosed a set of the rules for you to review with your parents. Although you were not on a Laidlaw school bus, I am nonetheless pleased that your bus ride was enjoyable.

Sincerely,

Peter J. Settle
Vice President
Marketing, Student Transportation

PJS/trm

Enclosures
n:file\trs\naomi.doc

P.S. Be sure to review and learn the rules of school bus safety.

Ten Rules for School Bus Safety

1. Be at the bus stop early.
2. Wait for the bus in a safe place. — away from the road.
3. Take your seat right away.
4. Stay seated at all times.
5. Keep hands, arms and head inside the bus at all times.
6. Listen to the bus driver and follow directions.
7. Leave the bus carefully using the handrail.
8. Take 10 giant steps beyond front bumper.
9. Look both ways before crossing the road.
10. Keep away from the bus if you drop or forget something.

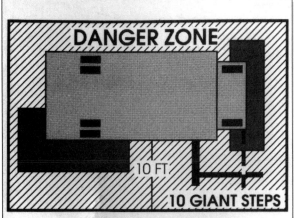

How To Cross Safely

1. *Avoid the danger zone!* Walk ten giant steps beyond the front bumper of the bus.

2. Stop! Wait for the driver's signal.

3. Check for traffic both ways.

4. Listen! If the driver blows the horn, go back.

5. Cross while continuing to check for traffic from both directions.

6. Walk straight across—not at an angle.

Dear God,

I'm having a new baby sister. Thank you for making her. I hope she looks like me. Can you make the baby come sooner?

Love,

Naomi

Naomi wrote to God because she had news of extreme importance. We got a reply nine months later.

Dear Beanie Baby Company,

First I had eight Beanies. Then my brother gave me two. Now I have ten. Why don't you make people Beanies? Why don't you make clothes for them?

Love,

Naomi

P.S. My friends have more than me.

No reply.

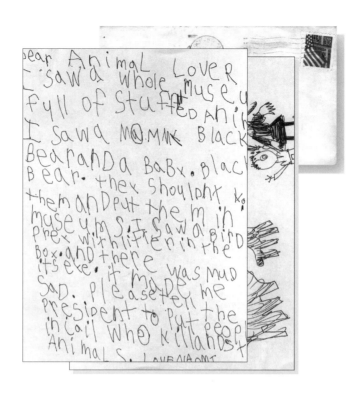

Dear Animal Lover,

I saw a whole museum full of stuffed animals. I saw a mommy black bear and a baby black bear. They shouldn't kill them and put them in museums. I saw a bird of prey with litter in the box. And there was mud in its eye. It made me sad. Please tell the president to put people in jail who kill and stuff animals.

Love,

Naomi

Naomi visited a science museum and was troubled at the sight of stuffed wild animals. She seemed to appreciate the displays for giving her a close-up look at indigenous species, but was concerned that the animals' lives might have been sacrificed for the sake of wildlife exhibits—ironically enough, even one on pollution. Like many children her age, Naomi has a keen interest in nature, heightened a bit, perhaps, because we live next to the Chattahoochee River and count among our neighbors the geese and goslings who make their home there.

United States Department of the Interior

FISH AND WILDLIFE SERVICE
Washington, D.C. 20240

IN REPLY REFER TO:
FWS/EA

AUG - 8 1997

Ms. Naomi Shavin
980 Edgewater Drive
Atlanta, Georgia 30328

Dear Ms. Shavin:

We received your father's letter with your original letter and drawing on hunting. We don't know what happened to your earlier letter, but we did not see it. While we respect your opinion about mounted animals in museums, hunting is legal all across the United States. There is a difference, however, between legal hunting and illegal killing and poaching of wildlife. Both State and Federal officers actively pursue people who hunt illegally. They are arrested, jailed and fined. But legal hunters have a right to pursue game and to mount the animals they shoot. I have enclosed a fact sheet on hunting that explains these issues in greater depth and also discusses the important role hunters play in conservation.

Sincerely,

Dan Ashe
Assistant Director - External Affairs

Attachment

YOU ASKED ABOUT HUNTING

Hunting wild animals has been a way of life for mankind throughout history. The hunting of deer, bear, ducks, and other animals has provided people with food, clothing, and shelter for centuries. Without the meat and skins provided by wild animals, the American colonists would not have been able to survive the difficult, early years in this country. The valuable hides of furbearers that were hunted and trapped, such as beaver, fox, otter, lynx, and pine marten, were critical to the survival and livelihood of many settlers in the New World.

Today, some people believe that hunting is wrong because killing and eating wild animals is no longer necessary for survival. They point out that plenty of food is available in supermarkets. But millions of Americans continue to hunt. Some people hunt to feed their families, and many do so because they enjoy the tradition, the outdoor experience, and the sense of being a part of nature.

Hunting today is strictly regulated by state and federal governments. Wildlife managers use hunting as a tool to help conserve and manage wildlife habitat and populations. In addition, hunting also provides billions of dollars annually to the economy.

Personal Enjoyment

There are many personal rewards that give hunting a special character, place, and value as part of America's heritage. Hunting is a unique way for an individual to interact with nature, and helps a person learn about the outdoors. Hunting is an outdoor activity that can be enjoyed together by husbands and wives, parents and children.

New friendships and a sense of good sportsmanship can arise from a day spent hunting. It also provides an opportunity to engage in good physical exercise and refresh one's mind and spirits. Many people consider game, such as a wild goose, rabbit, pheasant, or deer, to be a delicacy.

Wildlife Management

Hunting is also used as a tool to help manage wildlife. For example, deer can become so numerous that there is not enough food for all of them, especially during the winter. Without hunting to reduce their numbers, many would starve or become sick. A herd of hungry deer can quickly strip the vegetation that provides them and other animals with food and cover.

Too many deer can also lead to auto accidents when they cross highways in search of food. Deer may also damage property by eating corn or fruit trees because there is not enough natural vegetation for them to eat in the forest.

Hunting deer, bear, ducks, and other animals has provided people with food, clothing, and shelter for centuries.

Outbreaks of disease can occur when wild animals become too plentiful. For instance, small carnivores such as raccoons and foxes are susceptible to rabies and distemper, which can be transmitted to cats, dogs, farm animals, and even people.

Benefits to Society

Hunters have been the backbone of wildlife conservation programs in the United States. Because hunters spend time in the outdoors and learn about animals and their habitats, they are strong supporters of programs to help conserve wildlife and the environment.

Many people do not realize that hunters also provide a major source of funding for wildlife conservation. Hunting license fees support the management, law enforcement, research, and educational programs of state wildlife agencies.

Federal excise taxes on guns, ammunition, and archery equipment provide more than $100 million each year. These funds are annually distributed to the states by the U.S. Fish and Wildlife Service to support state wildlife conservation and hunter education programs.

Federal Migratory Bird Hunting and Conservation Stamps (commonly called Duck Stamps), purchased mostly by waterfowl hunters, provide about $20 million annually to buy wetlands habitat for the National Wildlife Refuge System. Since 1934, more than 4.2 million acres of refuge lands have been acquired with Duck Stamp revenues.

Hunting also supports many businesses and provides an extra source of income for farmers who lease their land to hunters. According to a survey by the U.S. Fish and Wildlife Service, in 1991 hunters spent nearly $9 billion on transportation, food, lodging, and special equipment.

Hunting: A Personal Choice

Many people oppose hunting because they think it causes animals to become endangered. Large-scale, uncontrolled commercial or "market" hunting that occurred in this country in the 19th and early 20th centuries did imperil animals like the buffalo. Today, hunting regulations are set each year by federal and state wildlife agencies

Federal Duck Stamps, purchased mostly by waterfowl hunters, provide about $20 million annually to buy wetlands habitat for the National Wildlife Refuge System. To date, more than $450 million in Duck Stamp revenues has been used to purchase more than 4.2 million acres of wetlands for the refuge system.

and are enforced by conservation officers, often called *game wardens*. In addition, biologists study hunted species, such as waterfowl, and if their numbers become too low for any reason, hunting is further restricted or even prohibited. In general, hunting regulations are designed to ensure hunters' harvests are compatible with each game species' ability to sustain viable numbers.

Wildlife biologists today agree that legal hunting is not a threat to our wildlife. The real threat to wildlife is destruction of habitat—forests, wetlands, and other wild places animals need for food and cover. No species can survive if it has no place to feed, rest, and rear its young.

Some people would never dream of killing a wild animal. Others believe that hunting is a natural part of the human tradition. Whether or not to hunt is a personal decision. But if hunters and nonhunters will respect each other's choices and work together on behalf of wildlife, we can preserve America's rich natural heritage for future generations to enjoy.

Illustrations by Robert Savannah

Because hunters spend time in the outdoors and learn about animals and their habitats, they are strong supporters of programs to help conserve wildlife and the environment.

BIOLOGUE SERIES

Prepared by:
U.S. Department of the Interior
U.S. Fish and Wildlife Service
1995

Dear Eskimoes,

What is it like there? Are there any wolves? Are you friends with any wolves? Is there a queen or anything?

If you ever want to be warm, come to Atlanta. The dogwood trees are blooming and the Chinese wisteria are everywhere.

Spring comes in like a lion and comes out like a sheep.

Love,

Naomi

Naomi wanted to write to "the eskimoes." On the Internet, I found a website for a school in the northern-most school district in Alaska. One of the teachers there hailed from Alabama. I figured that a fellow Southerner wouldn't mind answering the questions of a Georgia kindergarten student.

4-16-97

Dear Naomi,

    I was happy to get a letter from a little Georgia peach. I grew up in Arlington, near Albany. I have lots of relatives in the Atlanta area. I know about spring there because I have an uncle in Marietta that emails me about the flowers and warm weather (kind of cool right now). I tell him about our weather here (no flowers, not even a tree).

    Our kindergarten teacher and students kindly answered your letter. We hope you enjoy the reply.

    Now, you have to do a favor for me. Go outside, take a deep breath of spring air and say "Ahhhh." That one will be dedicated (oops) to your new friend (lonesome for the south) in Point Lay!

Love,
Dianne Talyor
dtalyor @ NSBSD
dtalyor@arctic.nsbsd.k12.ak.us

Dear Naomi Shavin,

We received your nice letter and pictures. They are really good. You really write a nice letter.

I am the Kindergarten teacher here at Cully School. My friend Dianne Talyor asked if my students would like to do something for you. So we drew pictures. I stand in front of the class, we decide what we are drawing, and then they follow directions. I am sending all of their pictures that they drew. They wanted to be neat and do a nice job for you.

We do have wolves here. They rarely come through the village. I have only seen tracks of them. They really have large paws. People do hunt the wolves once in awhile. So there are wolf skins. People use the wolf fur in their ruffs for their parkas. (parka is an Eskimo word) I do not know if there are queens in the packs. They do live together in a pack and have a leader.

We have had some polar bear come into the village. These are very frightening. If they can't get the polar bear to leave the village, they have to kill it. The Eskimo people do eat polar bear meat. It has to be cooked for a very long time. You can easily get trichinosis from it, if it isn't cooked properly. About six years ago, a young man and his girlfriend were out walking in the very early hours of the day. A polar bear came after them. Rhoda ran into the nearest house, but Carl was killed and eaten. The bear was starving and was desperate. It has really been scary. We see tracks of polar bear around town, too. They usually go after dogs.

This village is very small. There are ten blocks in this village. There are about 200 people. 105 of the 200 are children. Some people have large families. Some houses have more than one family living in it.

The school has about 80 students. We teach three and four year olds through the twelfth grade. When my husband and I moved here twelve years ago, there were 28 students in the school. So you can see the school has grown.

It is very cold here. The wind blows most of the time and blows very hard. Around Christmas, it is usually about 50 degrees below zero. Then with the wind chill factor, it is about 150 degrees below zero. We dress very warmly. The Eskimo parkas are nice and warm, if they have fur lining. A lot of people wear goggles over their eyes, cover their nose and mouth with scarves, to keep from getting frost bitten. I do know some men who have lost fingers and toes due to freezing. So it is vital to wear the proper clothing.

We have no trees here. There are willow bushes along the river near here. The mountains are about 60 miles away and there are no trees there either. We are a couple hundred miles away from the Arctic Circle.

There is beauty here. The sky can be a wonderful blue. The sunsets are outstanding. And the tundra is beautiful in the fall.

The Eskimo hunt for beluga whales here in July. They need about thirty of them for a year. When they start swimming by in herds, the Eskimo go out in their boats and herd them into the lagoon. Then they slaughter them and butcher them. They are stored in "ice cellars".

In other villages, the people go whaling for bowhead whales. These can be very large. Each village is allocated a certain number of whales that they can get (or strike). If they "strike" a whale and the whale can't be caught, it is counted against them.

These Eskimos do not use igloos. They use tents when they go hunting. They have certain camp sites that they have used for years. They fish and hunt while at camp. It must be very enjoyable and quiet for them. A lot of them take radios with them so they can get news from home and send messages back home.

The people use the gym every day. During the day, each class has a time to use it. Then in the evenings, they also have a time to use it. Adults use it each evening. They play a lot of basketball. We have tricycles for them to use in the gym. They roller blade, too. We have allot of different equipment for them to use. We have had cross country skis for them to use outside. They are finally getting an outside playground this summer. They have a ball game that they use a ball and bat. It really isn't much like the way we play baseball in the "lower 48". They have a wonderful time.

The Eskimo love to have a good time. They joke around a lot and enjoy each other. The women still tend to the skins and sew skins into parkas and boots (mukluks). They make wonderful hats and gloves, too. I can't forget the slippers, too. There are men who carve walrus ivory into many different things. These are wonderful. The men, also, make baskets out of baleen. There are some women who make a toy called a "yoyo". They, also, make dolls that are wonderful.

We have total darkness in November until the end of January here in Point Lay. Right now we have sunshine until 10:30 P.M. (Long days) They will have 24 hours of sunshine before very long.

I hope this has answered some of your questions.

I will explain the pictures that we drew.

1. Eskimo girl
2. Eskimo boy
3. igloo (which is just a word for house)
4. Skido
5. Ulu (Eskimo knife)
6. tent for camping (with a stove inside)
7. skin boat for whaling (made of seal skin sewn together a certain way so they won't leak)
8. Cargo sled. These are more sturdy and used behind a skido to haul stuff to and from camp. You see very few basket sleds here in the far north. They need something more sturdy for this rough tundra.

Our school is over on May 9. The villagers want their children out of school so they can hunt. The birds really come in here in the summer. They actually are starting back now.

Sincerely yours

Mrs. Kay Hammond

Dear Rabbi Goodman,

Shalom.

Are any Chinese people Jewish?

What does God look like? What does he talk like? Was he ever a child?

How do prayers get to heaven?

Love,

Naomi

The really, really tough questions go to Naomi's rabbi, who favors her with thoughtful replies, leavened with humor. During the Jewish holiday of Passover, children are taught to ask the traditional four questions. Naomi added five more for the rabbi's consideration.

RABBI ARNOLD M. GOODMAN

AHAVATH ACHIM SYNAGOGUE
600 PEACHTREE BATTLE AVENUE, N.E.
ATLANTA • GEORGIA 30327
404-355-5222

April 14, 1997
8 Nisan 5757

Dear Naomi,

Thank you for the beautiful pictures. I enjoy looking at them.

Now to answer your questions:
There are Chinese people who are Jewish. Some of them live in China and some live in the United States. You can be Jewish if you are African American or Chinese or even Native American.

We don't know what God looks like. What makes God different is that He has no body or shape, but is a spirit Who is everywhere at the same time. God can do things that no human being can do.

God was never a child. He sort of has been the way He is, all His life.

Our prayers get to heaven by our voices. When we pray we speak to God and He hears us. He may not always want to do what we ask Him to do, but He does hear us.

I hope this answers some of your questions, and if you have a chance to draw another picture for me, I would like to have it.

Please give your mommy and daddy a kiss for me.

Sincerely yours,

RABBI ARNOLD M. GOODMAN

AMG: bo

Naomi Shavin
980 Edgewater Drive
Atlanta, Georgia 30328

HAPPY PESACH

Dear Comet Watcher,

I've been watching the Hale-Bopp comet for days to see if it's still here. We saw a lunar eclipse. Me and my daddy went late, late at night and didn't tell Mommy.

I've been learning about the planets in school. You cannot live on the sun because it is too hot. And Pluto is too cold.

Can you invite my family and me to find a comet named after us?

Love,

Naomi

Naomi became interested in the stars after we began making nightly treks to the bottom of the driveway to catch a glimpse of the Hale-Bopp comet. She was eager to correspond with someone who knew more about these things than her dad.

Harvard-Smithsonian Center for Astrophysics

60 Garden Street, Cambridge, MA 02138

4/8/97

Dear Naomi —

I am glad you're enjoying the comet.

I thought you might like to see what it looks like where I work, so I'm sending you these booklets.

Good luck with your observations.

Alyssa A. Goodman, Ph.D '89
Assoc. Prof. of Astronomy.

HARVARD COLLEGE OBSERVATORY
Established 1839

SMITHSONIAN ASTROPHYSICAL OBSERVATORY
Established 1890

Dear Earthquake Scientist,

I know what earthquakes are. It's when the earth has cracks in it and people can fall in. It happens when the earth moves and goes too far apart and there's cracks.

My mom is like an earthquake. My dad is like lightning and thunder. My brother is like wind and rain. I am like a willow that gets sucked up in a tornado.

How can you tell when an earthquake is coming?

Love,
Naomi

20 June 1997

Dear Naomi,

Thank you for your nice note in which you talk about earthquakes.

You ask how we can tell if an earthquake is coming. Alas... we usually get very little warning. We are trying to learn as much as we can so that we can do better about warning people.

I am living in Virginia. 100 years ago we had an earthquake that was felt in many states – but no people were harmed. I am including an article published in the Roanoke Times about this earthquake.

I hope you are having a good summer!

Sincerely yours,

Arthur Snoke

Dear Lightning Bug Lover,

Families of fireflies have different lights so they know whose family is whose. So the children and the fathers can find their families. Me and my dad are going to catch fireflies this summer. We are going to use a butterfly net and a flashlight. We turn it off and on, off and on, off and on.

How do you know when they come out?

God put a special little light in their tushy so they can light up.

Love,

Naomi

If there were no such things as lightning bugs, drowsy children would invent them to bring their summer dreams to life. Naomi's letter went to one of the leading lights in the field of bioluminesence.

Department of Biochemistry and Molecular Biology
246B Noble Research Center
Stillwater, Oklahoma 74078-3035
405-744-6189

May 28, 1997

Ms Naomi Shavin
980 Edgewater Drive NW
Atlanta, Georgia 30328

Dear Naomi,

Thank you very much for your letter and the drawing of your family on a firefly collection trip. Yes, I do love fireflies. I can remember as a small child collecting them in Texas where I grew up. And here some 60 years afterward I have been studying them in the laboratory for some 20 happy years. There are many things still to be learned.

Fireflies appear in Oklahoma in late spring - May to June. The exact time depends on how warm it has been and how much rain. I do not know the correct range of combinations. But they do seem to like wet and warm weather. Sometimes they will appear again in late August and September. This requires a cooler time and rain and does not always occur.

There is one family (species) of fireflies that we have studied in detail. They only come out after dark and then can fly for most of the night. They fly higher and faster than the usual ones.

My grandchildren have helped me collect fireflies for our studies. I still collect them and also just watch their beautiful lights. I was glad to see that your dog helps you.

I hope that you continue to study fireflies because there is so much more to learn about them. They are very important in helping with medical and environmental research.

My colleague Dr. Ford recognized that your were Jewish as she is.

I am sending a couple of reprints that you may want to save and read in a few years. I have some special keepsakes that I received as a child and now realize how special they are. Also there is a key-chain light.

Keep up your study.

Love and flashes,

Franklin R. Leach

The Campaign for OSU

I read Professor Leach's wonderful letter to Naomi over and over. The firefly key-chain was a special treat. Naomi could not wait to see what was inside the bulky envelope and was delighted to receive the keepsake.

Dr. Ford is right; Naomi is Jewish. I wonder what gave it away—the Jewish stars in the night sky in Naomi's drawing or the vernacular of the letter?

It takes considerable effort for a five-year-old to write a letter, even when she has her dad's help. Responses like this are a reward for Naomi's effort. She wrote a thank you note to show her appreciation.

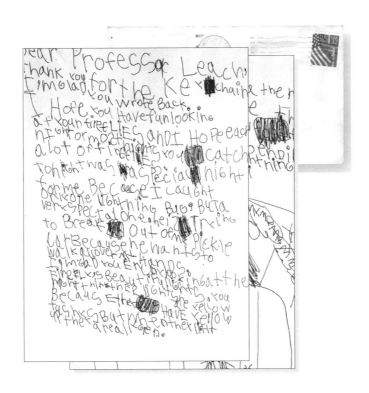

Dear Professor Leach,

Thank you for the keychain. I'm glad you wrote back. I hope you have fun looking at your fireflies and I hope each night or most nights you catch a lot of fireflies.

Tonight was a special night for me because I caught only one lightning bug, but a very special one. He is trying to break out of my pickle jar because he wants to walk all over my hands.

I'm glad you enjoy looking at the firefly's beautiful lights. You might think their lights are yellow because they have yellow tushies, but when they light up they are really green. In one tiny little area there is a little bulb with fire that has green and yellow food coloring in it.

I'm sending a picture of me, my lightning bug, and my keychain.

Love and flashes,

Naomi

Dear Reptile House,

I like poisonous snakes. They're interesting. I like turtles and crocodiles and scenes of life.

What do the snakes eat?

Snapping turtles aren't afraid of anything except God's voice.

Love,

Naomi

In my cover letter, I mentioned how much Naomi and I love the reptile house at Zoo Atlanta. Her mother won't step foot in the place. During our summer visits Naomi and I spend considerable time there while her mother wilts in the afternoon sun. Maybe we just like it because it's cool inside.

ZOO ATLANTA

Dear Naomi,   April 22, 1997

        Thanks for your letter of interest.
We like getting responses from the public.
It is wonderfull that you have taken interest in reptiles,
we, you and all of us here, are a rare breed.
Your note is now hanging up in our Kitchen.
Please, Next time your in, say Hello.

        Take care and share your enthusiam with others.

                                        Take care,

                                        Todd, Kelsey, Fred,
                                        Howard, sue, and mike

Conservation Leadership For Our Second Century
800 Cherokee Avenue, S.E., Atlanta, Georgia 30315 (404) 624-5600
Fax# (404) 627-7514 Telex 430-189

ACCREDITED
AMERICAN ASSOCIATION
OF ZOOLOGICAL
PARKS AND AQUARIUMS

RECYCLED PAPER

Mark and Naomi Shavin
980 Edgewater Drive NW
Atlanta, GA 30328

Dear Reptile Enthusiasts,

Todd is our newest reptile keeper and was enthusiastic to answer
your letter. What he was trying to say was:

Most snakes eat mice, rats and other small mammals, but
there are over two thousand species of snakes which may eat anything
from centipedes to other snakes. No snake eats any plant material,
however. King cobras and kingsnakes (kingsnakes are found here in
Georgia) are two kinds of snakes that eat other snakes. One snake,
the scarlet snake, also found in Georgia, eats mostly eggs from other
reptiles.

Thank you again for taking the time to write to us. We're glad
people share our interest in reptiles.

Also the drawings were excellent.

Thanks again,

Michael Fost
Reptile Keeper

P.S. This has been an attempt at humor. We hope you enjoyed it.

ACCREDITED
AMERICAN ASSOCIATION
OF ZOOLOGICAL
PARKS AND AQUARIUMS

Conservation Leadership For Our Second Century

800 Cherokee Avenue, S.E., Atlanta, Georgia 30315 (404) 624-5600
Fax# (404) 627-7514 Telex 430-189

RECYCLED PAPER

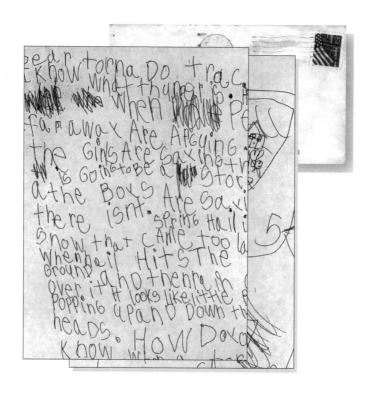

Dear Tornado Tracker,

I know what thunder is. It's when people far away are arguing. The girls are saying, "There is going to be a storm," and the boys are saying, "There isn't."

Spring hail is snow that came too late.

When hail hits the ground and then rain comes over it, it looks like little bunnies popping up and down their heads. How do you know when a tornado is coming? Have you ever been near a tornado?

Love,

Naomi

While driving with Naomi and her brother Adam, we got caught in a terrific hail storm. It prompted some amusing observations and a letter to the National Severe Storms Laboratory in Norman, Oklahoma.

U.S. DEPARTMENT OF COMMERCE
National Oceanic and Atmospheric Administration
ENVIRONMENTAL RESEARCH LABORATORIES

NOAA/NSSL
1313 Halley Circle
Norman, OK 73069   R/E/NS
(405) 366-0499
(405) 366-0472 (FAX)
Internet: brooks@nssl.noaa.gov

7 August 1997

Miss Naomi Shavin
980 Edgewater Drive NW
Atlanta, GA 30328

Dear Naomi,

Thank you very much for your letter. I'm sorry I didn't write back sooner, but I've been out of town a lot lately. I have a daughter named Sarah who's the same age as you are and we talk about storms a lot when they're around here. I'm going to share your explanations of thunder and hail with her. She'd like to tell you she knows that the safest place to be in a bad storm is in the middle of our house on the lowest floor, and she hopes that you'll make sure your family does the same thing.

We know when tornadoes are coming by using some special machines and by having people who are trained to go out and watch for them. The machines are called radars and they help us see what is going on inside of storms. With them, we can see where and how hard it's raining or hailing and, with some of the radars, we can see how the wind is blowing inside the storm. With this kind of information, we can usually do a pretty good job of knowing where and when tornadoes will happen.

I've seen about 15-20 tornadoes. The closest I've ever been has been about 1/4 mile. I don't think you should try to see tornadoes. I can be safe doing it because I know how storms act and what they're probably going to do. That way, I can keep myself and my family safe if we're out watching storms. The safest thing to do though is to stay out of their way!

You wrote a very nice letter and I hope that you continue to ask questions. I'm a scientist and one of the most important parts of my job is asking good questions. It's the best way to learn!

Sincerely,

Harold

Harold E. Brooks
Meteorologist
Head, NSSL Mesoscale Applications Group

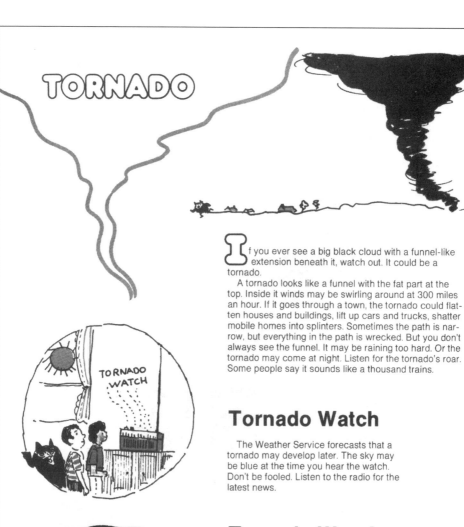

TORNADO

If you ever see a big black cloud with a funnel-like extension beneath it, watch out. It could be a tornado.

A tornado looks like a funnel with the fat part at the top. Inside it winds may be swirling around at 300 miles an hour. If it goes through a town, the tornado could flatten houses and buildings, lift up cars and trucks, shatter mobile homes into splinters. Sometimes the path is narrow, but everything in the path is wrecked. But you don't always see the funnel. It may be raining too hard. Or the tornado may come at night. Listen for the tornado's roar. Some people say it sounds like a thousand trains.

Tornado Watch

The Weather Service forecasts that a tornado may develop later. The sky may be blue at the time you hear the watch. Don't be fooled. Listen to the radio for the latest news.

Tornado Warning

A tornado has been sighted. It may move toward you. Dark clouds boil in the sky.

There may be thunder and lightning and heavy rain. And there may be hail. When you see large hail, you may be close to a tornado. Seek shelter.

Power may go off. Funnels reach down from the black clouds.

8

What to do—
IN YOUR HOUSE—

- When you hear the <u>tornado watch</u>, keep your eye on the sky for signs of a possible tornado and listen to the radio for the latest advice from the National Weather Service. When you hear the <u>warning</u>, act to protect yourself.

- Get away from windows. They may shatter, and glass may go flying.
- Go the the basement. Get under a heavy workbench or the stairs.
- If there is no basement, go to an inside closet, bathroom, or hallway on the lowest level of the house.
- Get under a mattress. Protect your head.

Downtown or in a shopping mall...

- Get off the street.
- Go into a building, stay away from windows and doors.

Outside...

- Get out of a car and inside a house or building.
- Don't try to outrun a tornado in a car. Tornadoes can pick up a car and throw it through the air.
- If you're caught outside, lie in a ditch. Or crouch near a strong building.
- Cover your head with your hands.

9

IN SCHOOL

- Follow directions
- Go to an inside hall on the lowest floor.
- Crouch near the wall. Bend over with your hands on the back of your head.
- Keep away from glass and stay out of big rooms like the gym, cafeteria, or auditorium.
- Keep a battery radio on. Listen for news about the tornado.

If you live in a mobile home, get out. Even if it's tied down, a mobile home can be shattered by a tornado. The whole thing can be lifted up and dropped. Get out and into a safer place. Some mobile home areas have storm shelters. If you can't get to a shelter, lie in a ditch and cover your head with your hands.

And remember, when there's a tornado there can be a lot of lightning.
- Stay away from anything that uses electricity.
- Stay away from anything metal—faucets, radiators, sinks, and tubs.

Tornadoes are scary. They pack a lot of energy; enough to blow down a whole town. But you can live through a tornado. Don't panic Be smart. know what to do, and **do it.**

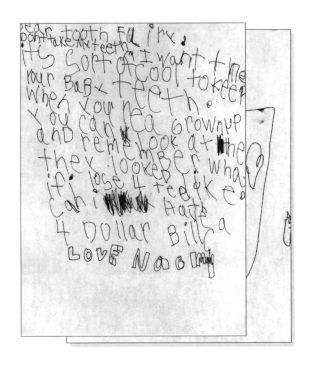

Dear Tooth Fairy,

Don't take my teeth. I want them.

It's sort of cool to keep your baby teeth. When you're a grownup you can look at them and remember what they looked like.

If I lose 4 teeth, can I have a 4-dollar bill?

Love,

Naomi

From The Office Of

THE TOOTH FAIRY

DEAR NAOMI,

I CAN'T BELIEVE YOU'VE ALREADY LOST TWO TEETH! YOU'RE GROWING UP SO FAST.

I LOVED YOUR LETTER. OF COURSE YOU CAN KEEP ANY TEETH THAT FALL OUT. JUST DON'T LET THEM BITE ANYONE! MANY CHILDREN LIKE TO KEEP THEIR TEETH TO REMEMBER WHAT IT WAS LIKE TO BE 5 YEARS OLD.

I HOPE WHEN YOU THINK BACK TO WHEN YOU WERE 5, YOU'LL REMEMBER THAT YOUR LITTLE BROTHER IS YOUR BEST FRIEND, YOUR MOTHER HAS THE SOFTEST ARMS AND YOUR FATHER IS YOUR PAL.

LOVE,

THE TOOTH FAIRY

P.S. BRUSH AND FLOSS YOUR TEETH BEFORE YOU GO TO THE DENTIST. THIS ALWAYS IMPRESSES THEM.

Dear Dreamers,

I don't like sleeping in my own bed. I miss my mommy and daddy. I call for them 10,000 times. I go running into their room because I'm afraid a monster is going to drop from the ceiling and a gorilla is going to throw a giant rock on me.

Once I had a nightmare about a 2-headed monster. What does it mean?

Love,

Naomi

P.S. If you want to know anything else, ask the Tooth Fairy.

Naomi falls asleep in her own room, but before long she is either begging her exhausted parents to come sleep in her room or streaking down the hallway like a rocket and hurling herself into our bed. I told Naomi she ought to share her sleep problem with "an expert," someone who could put her fears to rest, and then, perhaps, we'd all sleep better.

729 Fifteenth Street, NW

Fourth Floor

Washington, DC 20005

Telephone: (202) 347-3471

FAX: (202) 347-3472

E-mail: natsleep@erols.com

NATIONAL SLEEP FOUNDATION

May 29, 1997

Ms. Naomi Shavin
980 Edgewater Drive NW
Atlanta, GA 30328

Dear Naomi:

Thank you for writing to us at the National Sleep Foundation about your scary nightmares. Your letter and picture helped us to understand how frightened you are feeling!

You may feel better to know that your fears are sometimes shared by many other children. Sleep doctors suggest that your parents calm you down and put you back to bed holding something special to you like a stuffed animal, doll, or pillow that will help you keep the monsters and gorillas out of your dreams.

We hope that you will have a good night's sleep from now on.

Sincerely,

Heidi Wunder

National Sleep Foundation

P.S. We've included for your parents a helpful brochure on children & sleep and a list of sleep centers in your area.

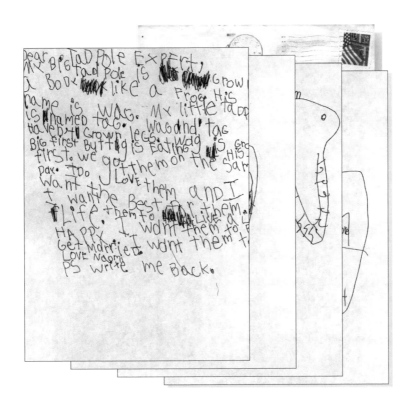

Dear Tadpole Expert,

My big tadpole is growing a body like a frog. His name is Wag. My little tadpole is named Tag. Wag and Tag haven't grown legs. Wag is growing big first, but Tag is eating his tail first. We got them on the same day.

I do love them and I want the best for them. I want them to live a long life. I want them to be happy. I want them to get married.

Love,

Naomi

P.S. Write me back.

Naomi is a real tadpole enthusiast. She is something of a tadpole herself. We sent her letter first to Wales to an expert in amphibian population dynamics. We had no particular connection to Wales other than an overweight Welsh corgi who kept eyeing the tadpoles and licking his chops. Hearing nothing, we sent the letter again, this time to the Tennessee Aquarium in Chattanooga.

Naomi's interest was piqued when we went to the mailbox to look for letters and instead found a frog in a puddle at the base of the driveway. She named him Spotty and was quite content until her little brother put the garden hose in his tank and the cold water gave him a chill from which he never recovered. We buried him in front of the house with a marker.

"What happens when a frog dies?" Naomi asked. "I wish there was no such thing as death in this world."

Later we bought a pair of tadpoles at the pet store, and a few months after that Naomi had a brief scare, believing one of them had died just on the cusp of full frog-hood. She called me at work, distraught and crying into the phone, "He never got to be a frog!" In fact, he was only pretending to be dead, and when I came home from work I took him downstairs, and he hopped across the kitchen floor.

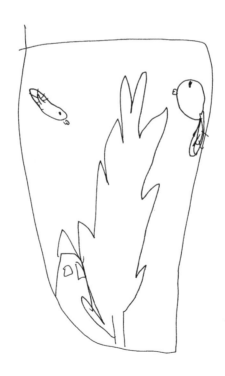

Tennessee Aquarium

Tim Schmiedehausen, Herpetologist (Tadpole Expert)
Tennessee Aquarium
One Broad Street
Chattanooga, TN 37401
Phone: 423/785-4084
Fax: 423/267-3561
E-mail: TGS@tennis.org

Dear Naomi,

Thank you for your letter and pictures of Wag and Tag. It is always nice to here from other people who love and care for their tadpoles.

It sounds like Wag and Tag are doing well and may soon become adult frogs. I have shared your experience many times by raising tadpoles myself. I have had frogs that have gotten married and had tadpoles and I have bought several types of frogs and tadpoles from pet shops just like you.

I am glad that you want the best and a long life for Wag and Tag but soon you will have to decide what to do when they become frogs. Once they are frogs you will have two choices, one is to keep them in a terrarium or let them go to live in the outdoors. A very important thing to know before releasing Wag and Tag is if they are truly a native species to your area! I am sure your father can help you with that question or your pet shop or you can also call me for this.

The other choice is to set up a terrarium for them and care for them in your home. This will require some reading of books and help from your parents so that Wag and Tags' home keeps them happy and comfortable. It will be some work, Naomi, if you decide to keep them inside but it can also be a very fun and rewarding experience.

I hope this letter is helpful to you in the care of Wag and Tag. Please let me know how everything works out with Wag and Tag.

Have you ever visited the Tennessee Aquarium Naomi? If you haven't I would like to invite you up to see all of our animals. We have fish, salamanders, snakes, turtles, and lots of frogs and toads. I hope I can meet you when you come by sometime!

Your Tadpole Friend,

Tim Schmiedehausen

P. O. Box 11048, Chattanooga, TN 37401-2048 Tel: 423-265-0695 Fax: 423-756-1849
Internet: http://www.tennis.org

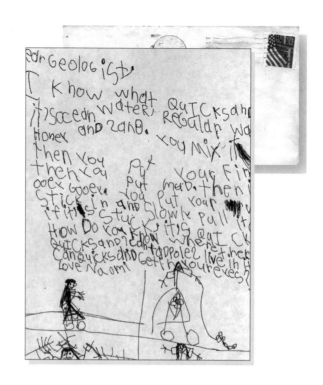

Dear Geologist,

I know what quicksand is. It's ocean water, regular water, honey, and sand. You mix it up. Then you put your finger in. Then you put mud. Then it's ooey-gooey. You put your worst stick in and slowly pull it out. If it's stuck, it's quicksand.

How do you know where there is quicksand? Can tadpoles live in it? Can quicksand get in your eyes?

Love,

Naomi

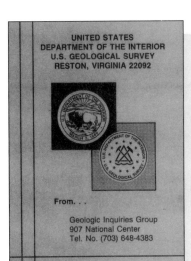

27 May 1997

Dear Mr. Shavin:

We recommend that you locate elementary reference materials on quicksand at your local library. Database searches of periodicals for children and general audiences are available to help you. Two elementary level reference books on quicksand are:

de Paola, Tomie, 1977, The Quicksand Book: New York, Holiday House, unpaginated.

Pearce, Q.L., 1989, Quicksand and Other Earthly Wonders: Englewood Cliffs, N.J, J. Messner, 64 p.

These books can be located in your local library or through the interlibrary loan program. Perhaps this will be an early opportunity to teach your child how to obtain information from the library.

These references discuss quicksand basics such as what makes up quicksand: sand (or a mixture of sand and larger or smaller particles) that is supersaturated with water under pressure from below. Some myths are also discussed. Quicksand does exist; however, very few people ever encounter it. Learning more about quicksand will help reduce your daughter's fears.

I hope that this is helpful.

Sincerely,

Diane Noserale
Geologist
Geologic Inquiries Group

Dear Grandpa Norman,
    I love you.
    I wish you were here to see Mommy have the new baby.
    My family is nice. They treat me great.
Love,
Naomi

Naomi experimented with different ways of writing letters. She wrote to her late Grandpa Norman in colored chalk on the driveway, believing he could look down from Heaven and read it.

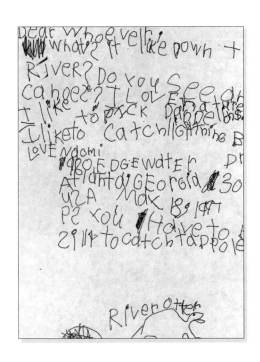

Dear Whoever,

What's it like down the river? Do you see any canoes?

I love nature. I like to pick dandelions. I like to catch lightning bugs.

Love,

Naomi

May 18, 1997

P.S. You have to be silly to catch tadpoles.

Naomi sat on the riverbank facing the water and penned a message to put inside a bottle. The bottle was clear, about ten inches tall, intended perhaps to hold kitchen spices or something as mundane as homemade salad dressing. We chose it for a more exotic fate and sealed Naomi's message inside with a cork and sturdy black tape. She tossed it into the Chattahoochee River, and I told her not to get her hopes up, that it could easily get tangled in underbrush or break open on a rock.

Naomi received a reply six months later. We had completely forgotten about her bottle, which ended up about one hundred miles downstream.

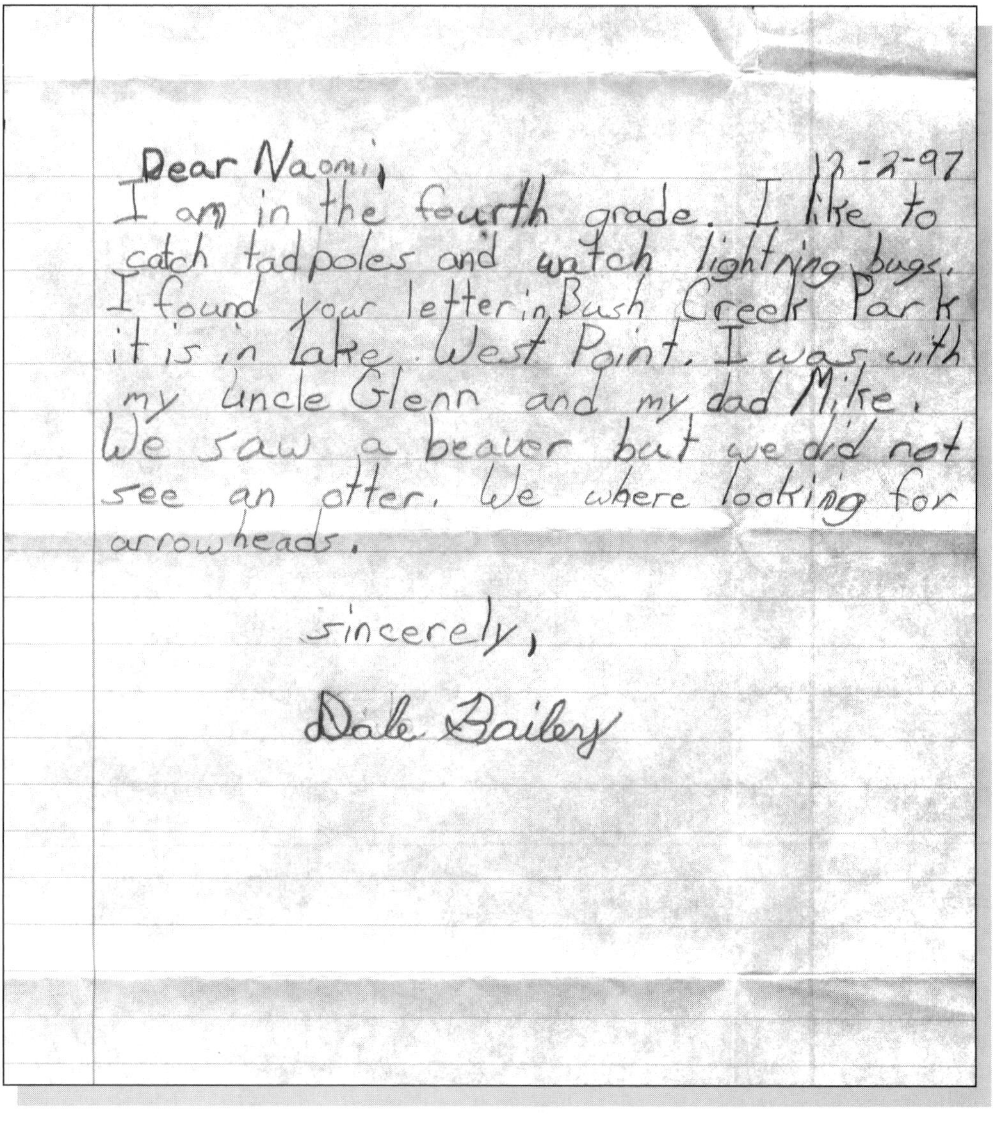

Dear Naomi,   12-2-97
I am in the fourth grade. I like to
catch tadpoles and watch lightning bugs.
I found your letter in Bush Creek Park
it is in Lake West Point. I was with
my uncle Glenn and my dad Mike.
We saw a beaver but we did not
see an otter. We where looking for
arrowheads.

            Sincerely,

            Dale Bailey

Dear Reverend Finster,

You do some good artwork.

I do art for a lot of reasons. I draw pictures of my family to remember when I was a child. I like the pictures I make.

If you would, could you draw me a picture of a tadpole? They're fascinating.

I'm giving you a picture I made.

Love,

Naomi

In kindergarten, children spend a lot of time finding creative ways to express themselves on paper—with pens, crayons, markers, paint. Naomi liked the idea of writing to a "real artist," so we studied a painting by Howard Finster and off went another letter.

Dear Naomi,
    Thank you for the painting Its very good for a little girl your age. Hope your parents will bring you to see the garden. I am not very good at drawing todpoles, Some day you may be a great Artist. Best Wishes to you in your art __ Sincerly
    Howard Finster

Finster Folk Art, #1 Hankins Drive, Summerville, GA 30747, 1-800-Finster

YOUR. TADPOLE BY Howard Finster

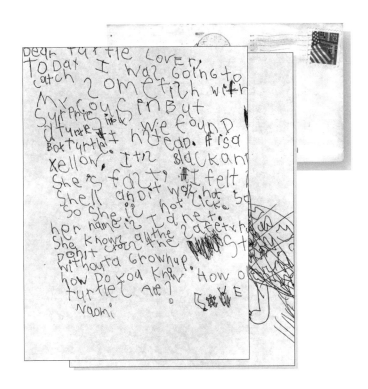

Dear Turtle Lover,

Today I was going to catch some fish with my cousin, but, surprisingly, we found a turtle instead. It is a box turtle. It's black and yellow. She's fast. I felt her shell and it was not soft, so she is not sick.

Her name is Janet. She knows all the safety rules. Don't cross the street without a grownup.

How do you know how old turtles are?

Love,

Naomi

Veterinary Associates - Stonefield

10466 Shelbyville Road
Louisville, Kentucky 40223
(502) 245-7863

5/29/97

DR. SAM VAUGHN
AVIAN SPECIALIST
ABVP, AVIAN DIPLOMAT
ASSOCIATION OF AVIAN VETERINARIANS

DR. KURT OLIVER
ASSOCIATION OF AVIAN VETERINARIANS

Dear Naomi:

Thank you for your letter!
I hope Janet is doing well and
she will appreciate being returned
to the wild. Turtles are hard to
age so I am sorry I do not
know how old Janet is by your
letter. Fishing is my favorite
hobby so good luck on your
next trip.

Sincerely,

Sam Vaughn

96

Dear Name Studier,

How come children don't have their mommy's last name?
I wish I had Mommy's last name when Daddy makes me mad.
I feel like I could break all the windows in the house and I
could smash all the mirrors to a 100 pieces.

I don't like when I brush my teeth and my dad brushes
my hair. It distracts me. When I wanted Froot Loops, my
daddy gave me Lucky Charms. I got really angry, but I had
to eat them.

My last name is Shavin. My mommy's last name is
Citron. If I had Mommy's last name, I'd always forget it.

Love,

Naomi

ASSOCIATION OF JEWISH GENEALOGICAL SOCIETII

P. O. Bo

Cabin John, Maryland 20818-(

20 October 1997,

Dear Mark Shavin

President
Sallyann Amdur Sack, Ph.D.
Maryland

Vice President
Karen Franklin
New York

Secretary
Saul Issroff
England

Treasurer
Hal Bookbinder
California

Member at large
Bruce Kahn
New York

Member at large
Howard Margolis
Georgia

Member at large
Arline Sachs
Virginia

Member at large
Lawrence Tapper
Canada

Past President
Robert Weiss
California

Your daughter's letter has been passed to me , as secretary of the AJGS, for reply. Apologies for the delay, but we have had a change of committee and the transit of mail has entailed some delays. In addition, we are all volunteers and have to fit in an enormous amount of work. The letter from your daughter is one of the more unusual ones.

I trust this reply will suffice.

Yours sincerely

Saul Issroff

Societies in: Argentina, Australia, Azerbaijan, Brazil, Canada, France, Germany, Israel,
Netherlands, South Africa, Sweden, Switzerland, United Kingdom, and United States

Dear NAOMI

I am writing to you on a   computer.
Thank you for writing to us. Your letter is very nice. Your name comes from the bible and was the name of the mother in law of a lady called RUTH in the Bible story. It comes from the Hebrew words that mean " beautiful, pleasant, good and delightful" . (From Kollatch, A. 'These are the Names'). Ruth was the wife of a man called Khilyon. He was the son of Elimelech and Naomi. Ruth was not born Jewish, but converted to become Jewish (I know this is a little difficult for a five year old!). King David was a descendant of this family.

This is a family

Your brother ADAM is named after the first man mentioned in   the
Bible story, called ADAM. And this is the Hebrew word for a   man
or a person.

I do not know the name of your new sister but I am sure it is also a nice name.

Your father's name , MARK, is from a Latin name, Marcus. This comes from the name Mars, the Roman God of War.

The surname, or second name of SHAVIN , is similar to Saviner and may mean that the family originally came from a small town called Sava in Gorki district of Russia, or Drissa in Latviaor Orsha or Gomel.

Your mother's surname ,CITRON, means a lemon in Yiddish. The name comes from places like Bialystok, Vladimir ,Lipovets and Kiev, Kishniev and Odessa. All these places are in Russia, Poland and the Ukraine. Your parents can show you these places on a map.

My name is SAUL, and I have a grandson called Daniel who is also five years old. He lives in Zurich in Switzerland and sometiems he comes to visit me in London and I take him to the ZOO and we see wild animals like LIONS. He has a sister who is two and her name is Jemma.

This is a picture of a doggie. Does it look like your doggie??

Best wishes.

Saul

Dear Gerber,

What is it like to make baby food? My mommy is going to have a new baby. The baby is going to be a girl and she will have my mommy's milk and then she'll have your baby food, but that's not the last step. Then she's going to have a birthday and she will turn one. I will be happy.

I love my new baby sister already though she isn't here. My new baby sister is coming in 6 weeks. I'm happy as can be. When she first comes out I will give her a great hug so she will know I am her sister and I will take care of her.

When I was a baby I ate your cut-up peas and apple-sauce so much. The new baby will like what I ate, I hope. Could you make chocolate-flavored baby food?

Love,

Naomi

Gerber   *Consumer Response*

GERBER PRODUCTS COMPANY • 445 STATE STREET • FREMONT, MICHIGAN 49413-0001

PHONE: (616) 928-2000

1-800-4-GERBER

June 17, 1997

Naomi Shavin
980 Edgewater Drive, N.W.
Atlanta, GA 30328

Dear Naomi:

Thank you for your recent letter and for your interest in Gerber Products Company. We welcome an opportunity to write to you.

We were pleased to learn that you will shortly have a new baby at your house. This is a time of great joy and the beginning of many changes in all of your lives.

We are taking this opportunity to send some materials we feel your mother will find useful and informative both now and after the baby arrives. Also enclosed are some coupons for her to use the next time she shops.

We were especially pleased to learn that you ate our foods when you were a baby and also that your mother plans to use them for the new baby. Since our primary concern here at Gerber is the health and well-being of infants and small children, it makes our work more meaningful when someone takes the time to let us know that we have been helpful in the all-important task of feeding and caring for their little one.

Thank you again for taking the time to write to us. Do not hesitate to get in touch with us any time you have questions regarding our company or its products. Letters are always welcome, and our toll-free consumer information number, 1-800-4-GERBER, is a convenient way to contact us any time of the day or night.

Sincerely,

Sandra Arrasmith
Consumer Service Representative

Enclosures
2107669A

Babies are our business...®

RECYCLED PAPER

Dear Mrs. Edelman,

I really loved kindergarten. Kindergarten was great. I loved it more than anything else. I liked it for a zillion 129 reasons. I had fun writing. Math was the hardest thing on earth. I know you were just doing it so I'd learn more. My favorite thing was saying good morning to you. I loved writing my ABC's. I'll miss you Mrs. Edelman and I'll miss Mrs. Rabin too. I loved you both a lot and I'll miss having kindergarten because it was fun. When I go up to my next grade, I won't get to see you very often. Each day when I came home from school with my bag loaded with stuff to play with, I thought about what a wonderful day I had. When I went to your class on the first day of school, I was scared and I thought my best friend Ariel was mean, but it turned out that she was nice.

Love,

Naomi

It was the end of the school year—a time for summing up, for saying thanks, for looking ahead.

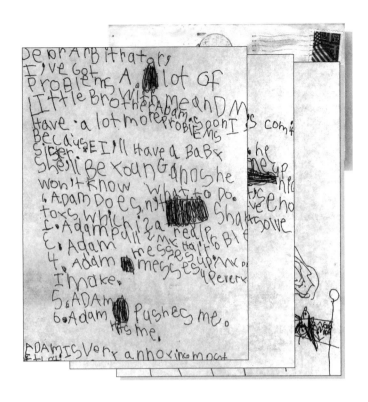

Dear Arbitrator,

I've got a lot of problems with me and my little brother Adam. Soon I'll have a lot more problems because I'll have a baby sister. She'll be young and she won't know what to do.

1. Adam doesn't share toys, which is a real problem.

2. Adam pulls my hair.

3. Adam messes up my dolls.

4. Adam messes up everything I make.

5. Adam pushes me.

6. Adam hits me.

7. Adam is very annoying most of the time, but sometimes he's loving and I don't mind.

Now that my little sister's coming, my brother sleeps in my room. He talks all the time. It keeps me up and I already have nightmares that keep me up and it's enough for me. Will you please try to solve my problems? If you can't solve all of them, then solve some.

Love and worries,

Naomi

My wife and I spend considerable time mediating disputes between Naomi and Adam. I tried to explain the difference between a judge and an arbitrator. I encouraged Naomi to lay out her grievances in a letter. We sent it to the Chairman of the National Labor Relations Board, who has been a member of the National Academy of Arbitrators for more than twenty-five years and has arbitrated and mediated more than two hundred labor disputes since 1965. I thought he might warm to the contest of wills my wife and I affectionately refer to as Naomi v. Adam.

William B. Gould IV
Chairman

September 24, 1997

Miss Naomi Shavin
980 Edgewater Drive NW
Atlanta, GA 30328

Dear Naomi:

Thank you for writing to me about your problems with your brother Adam. I have three children of my own, and when they were little they sometimes had disagreements like yours and Adam's.

Although I am an arbitrator I am not sure I can solve the problems between you and Adam, but here are a few suggestions. Since you are older than Adam and more grown up you have a special leadership responsibility to show him the way. Maybe if you are always willing to share your toys with Adam and never hit him or pull his hair he will learn by your good example. The more kindness and love you show toward him the more he will be likely to treat you the same way. But don't expect this to work every time, because it will take him a while to learn by your good example.

I enjoyed your letter and the picture you sent along with it. And I hope you and Adam and your new sister -- when she comes -- get along fine.

Sincerely yours,

William B. Gould IV
Chairman

107

Dear Vice-President Gore,

I wish you were the President and I'm sorry you're not. Being the President makes the rules. Being the Vice-President might not be that much fun, but it's still good, because if the President is really, really sick, then you can be the President. But I don't know if you can put your feet up on the table.

What's it like to be the Vice-President?
Love for you to be the President,
So love,
Naomi

THE VICE PRESIDENT
WASHINGTON

July 29, 1997

Ms. Naomi Shavin
980 Edgewater Drive NW
Atlanta, Georgia 30328-3510

Dear Ms. Shavin:

Thank you for writing to me with your questions and comments. I always am pleased to hear from young Americans, like you, who are learning about our government and current events in school.

Often, students ask me about my duties as Vice President. Under the Constitution, the Vice President has been given two formal roles in our government. The first is to serve as the President of the Senate and to vote only in the case of a tie. The second is to assume the presidency if the President dies or for any other reason is unable to perform his duties. In addition, I have two jobs assigned to me through the passage of laws: to serve as a member of both the National Security Council and the Board of Regents of the Smithsonian Institution.

I became involved in public service because I believe strongly that one person can make a positive difference for others. As you continue your education, I hope you will think about ways that you can help make America a better place to live for all of us. I am confident that you, too, will become a leader and that you will have a very positive impact on everyone associated with you.

Again, thank you for letting me hear from you. I wish you every personal success in the future.

Sincerely,

Al Gore

AG/evk
Enclosure

Dear Princess Diana,

I heard about your dress sale. I saw a pink dress with a purple scarf and it made me want to get one for my mommy and me. I hope one day to have enough money to buy one of your dresses.

You are not a mean princess. You're giving the money to the cancer people. I'm sending two dollars for the people who have cancer. My Grandpa Norman had cancer. I'm sorry you didn't sell the dresses then, but I'm glad you did now so the other people won't die.

What do you like better, being a princess or a teacher? I had the nicest teacher. Her name is Mrs. Edelman.

Love,

Naomi

Like other little girls, Naomi is intrigued by princesses and castles. She also has an eye for fashion. I showed her pictures of Princess Diana in Newsweek *and* People *magazines and told her about Diana's dress auction and what was behind it. She loved the idea of writing to a real princess.*

KENSINGTON PALACE
LONDON W8 4PU

From: The Office of Diana, Princess of Wales

25th July, 1997

Dear Naomi,

    The Princess of Wales has asked me to thank you for your lovely letter and the picture which you drew so carefully.   It was very kind of you to enclose $2 and this will be forwarded to a cancer charity who will be most appreciative of such a thoughtful donation.

    The Princess was delighted that the recent auction of dresses in New York was so successful and that the charities concerned will now receive substantial funds, enabling them to continue helping those with particular needs.

This letter comes to you with very best wishes from the Princess of Wales.

Yours sincerely,

Mrs. Colin MacMillan

Dear Mrs. MacMillan,

I'm sorry Princess Diana died.

I'm sorry you're sad.

We were Princess Diana's friends, too.

Love,

Naomi

P.S. Think of happy thoughts.

Princess Diana died just a month after we heard from Kensington Palace. I wasn't sure how to break the news to Naomi, but I wanted her to hear it from me. When I told her, her face took on a look of great sadness and she sat very still on the bed.

"Daddy," she said, "can we visit her grave and bring flowers?"

Dear Sarah,

We all love you, Sarah. Adam loves you, too, but he says you smell like Crackerjacks.

I think you are very cute and you have beautiful eyes. They are the prettiest I have seen in all my years of living. You have the best mom and dad anybody ever had.

Love,

Naomi

Your new best friend

and big sister

Naomi wrote a letter, a keepsake, to her new baby sister.

Dear Mom,

   We are going to the pet store. Adam, Dad, and I are going to buy fish.

   Don't make the French toast until we get home.

Love,
Naomi

Naomi's note to her sleeping mother.

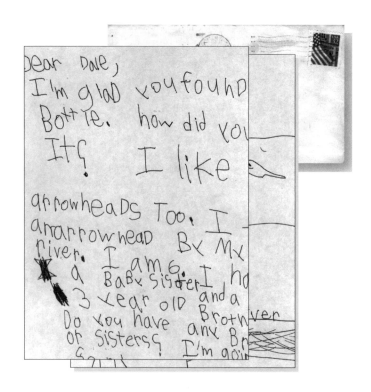

Dear Dale,

   I'm glad you found my bottle. How did you see it? I like arrowheads, too. I found an arrowhead by my river. I am 6. I have a baby sister and a 3-year-old brother. Do you have any brothers or sisters? I'm going to send you my picture. Will you send me yours?

Love,

Naomi

This is Naomi's letter back to Dale Bailey, the boy who found her message in a bottle.

Naomi, I heard about your book.
I have never writen to anybody before
until you. I would like to read your book
if I see some.
I haven't been looking for arrowheads in
a while. Sence it has been raining.
I have your letters in the envelopes
with my letter.
I have a picture of me in the letter.
What did you get for Christmas?
I got a beanbag to sit in and a air plane
on a string and a lot of other neat stuff.
I have to go now.

Sincerly,
Dale

117

Dear Bicycle Company,

My bike broke after the second time I rode it. It was a birthday present. My daddy took it back to the store.
I hope you make the bikes better so other children don't get broken bikes.
Love,
Naomi

DynaCraft Industries   **2550 Kerner St.**

San Rafael, CA 94901

December 31, 1997

Naomi Shavin
980 Edgewater Dr. NW

Atlanta, Georgia 30328

Dear Naomi:

We were very sorry to hear of your experience with the "Island Breeze". We hope that despite this experience you had a very delightful sixth birthday. We greatly appreciate your concern and will address the issue to further better our bikes. Again, thank you for taking the time and extra effort to write the letter and draw the picture that had alerted us to the problem with the "Island Breeze".

Sincerely,

David Martinez
Customer Service Representative

Dear 7Up,

Why do you put Christmas decorations on the 7Up boxes instead of Jewish decorations? Because I am Jewish I don't like it. I think you should put a rainbow on the boxes so there is no religions!

Love,

Naomi

P.S. I could have said put Jewish things, but the Christians would be left out and my babysitter Juanita is a Christian.

A year after Naomi wrote her first letter to the Coca-Cola Company about their holiday packaging, she noticed a box of 7Up in the pantry with a Christmas theme. It got under her skin.

Dr Pepper/Seven Up, Inc.
Corporate Communications, Consumer Affairs
P.O. Box 655086, Dallas, Texas 75265-5086
8144 Walnut Hill Lane, Dallas, Texas 75231-4372 • 214/360-7000

February 10, 1998

Naomi Shavin
980 Edgewater Drive N.W.
Atlanta, GA 30328

Dear Naomi:

We did not forget you! Your letter was addressed to the CEO, Todd Stitzer, who has many days of traveling away from his office. So he can see the letters addressed to him; we are sometimes late in replying. We do apology for the delay.

I checked with our promotion department about the 7 UP packaging. Gerald told me the Naughty or Nice promotion did have a Christmas theme using a string of lights. The string of lights was to project a festive atmosphere. We believe going with the commercial idea of using the lights did not show any type of religion.

Your letter gave us insight into a young lady who is showing great potential to start a career in letter writing. Enclosed is a coupon for a free purchase of 7 UP to enjoy with your family.

Sincerely,

Wynema Hamilton
Manager, Consumer Affairs

P.S. Naomi, do not forget tell your Dad we wrote back to you. Thanks.

Dear Treasury Secretary Rubin,

　　My allowance is 2 dollars. Do you think that is enough?

　　Your name is on every dollar bill. Do you write it or is it printed? Why is the money green? How do you spend your money?

Love,

Naomi

P.S. If I were in charge of the money, I would make it a triangle.

Naomi has begun to appreciate the importance of a dollar. Her interest in monetary policy was sharpened when her mother and I began paying her an allowance. She understands the concept of an allowance, but she's still a bit foggy on the notion of chores.

DEPARTMENT OF THE TREASURY
WASHINGTON, D.C. 20220

February 12, 1998

Naomi Shavin
980 Edgewater Drive, NW
Atlanta, GA 30328

Dear Naomi:

Thank you for your letter to Secretary Rubin. You asked about United States money. I am sorry it has taken so long to respond. We receive so much mail on the many issues for which the Treasury Department is responsible, we cannot reply as rapidly as we wish. I hope you understand and are still interested.

You will be interested to know, Naomi, that the United States Mint produces coins for general circulation, along with coins sold to collectors as numismatic items. The Mint has its headquarters in Washington, D.C., and produces an average of 52.5 million coins each day. While the Mint produces most of the coins in Philadelphia and Denver, it also produces some coins in San Francisco and West Point, New York.

The Bureau of Engraving and Printing (BEP), located in Washington, D.C., is responsible for designing and printing our paper currency. There is also a satellite production facility located in Fort Worth, Texas, which began operations in January 1991. Every day, the BEP prints approximately 22.5 million paper notes in denominations ranging from $1 to $100.

When the small currency notes in use today were first introduced in 1929, the Bureau of Engraving and Printing (BEP) continued using green ink. There were three reasons for this decision. First, pigment of that color was readily available in large quantity. Second, the color was high in its resistance to chemical and physical changes. Finally, the public psychologically identified the color green with the strong and stable credit of the Government. There is no definite reason green was chosen originally for our currency notes.

The BEP has researched this question and found some evidence to support the following explanation. It appears that the growing popularity of bank notes and the development of photography in the mid-1800's forced currency production changes. It was customary to print the currency notes in black combined with colored tints as a deterrent to counterfeiting. Early cameras saw everything in black and features that were distinguishable on a note by color variant lost their individuality when reproduced photographically. However, counterfeiters soon discovered that it was easy to remove the colored inks used then from a note without disturbing the black ink. In other words, a counterfeiter could erase the colored portion, photograph the black ink, and then make the desired number of copies. They then would overprint the copies with an imitation of the colored ink.

The solution to this problem was in the development of an ink that counterfeiters could not erase without adversely affecting the black coloring. After the development of such an ink, Tracy R. Edson purchased the patent rights. He was a co-founder of the American Bank Note Company. This was one firm that produced the first paper money issued by the United States. The companies printed the faces of these and other early notes under contract with a green tint, presumably of the protective ink.

When printing with oil-base inks, such as the "patent green," it is not unusual for the color to strike through to the opposite side of a sheet. It is possible that they used a darker shade of the ordinary green for the backs of the early currency notes to make the tine "strike through" less obvious.

The transition of printing money exclusively at the BEP was gradual. They probably printed the backs of the notes during the transition period in green simply to make all the currency a uniform color. Once the BEP was on full-scale production, there was no reason to change the traditional color and this practice remains to this day.

Enclosed is a series of fact sheets developed in our office explaining the various aspects of coin manufacture and distribution. I have also enclosed a BEP pamphlet explaining the production process for United States currency.

Thank you again for writing to Secretary Rubin. I hope this information is helpful to you.

Sincerely,

Dale M. Servetnick
Deputy Director, Office of Public Correspondence
dale.servetnick@treas.sprint.com
http://www.ustreas.gov/opc/

Enclosures

Dear Mr. Schulberg,

It's Sunday and I'm having a baked potato. I'm drinking milk. The first time I saw your "Got Milk" commercial I thought it said: "God Milk?"

I'm 6. I want to be in a "Got Milk" commercial. You should tell people to add things to their milk to make it taste better.

Love,

Naomi

Naomi brought up the "Got Milk?" advertising campaign. She said she didn't understand it at first. We sent her letter out to a couple of creative gurus.

Bozell

Bozell Worldwide, Inc.
Advertising
40 West 23rd Street
New York, New York 10010-5201
212-727-5053
Fax: 212-727-5799
E-mail: jschube@newyork.bozell.com

Jay Schulberg
Vice Chairman
Chief Creative Officer

November 20, 1997

Ms. Naomi Shavin
980 Edgewood Dr. NW
Atlanta, GA 30328

Dear Naomi,

Thank you very much for sending me your idea for "Got Milk." I think it is terrific.

Naomi, I am going to suggest that you send it to Jeff Goodby at:

Goodby, Silverstein & Partners
720 California St.
San Francisco, CA 94108

Jeff's advertising agency does the "Got Milk' campaign. We do the Milk Mustache campaign. They are both for milk, we just do different things. I have enclosed some Milk Mustache ads I think you would like.

Keep thinking of other big ideas like the one you sent me and keep drinking your milk.

With best wishes,

[signature]

enc.
/at

Now that we had the right contact, I sent a copy of Naomi's original letter to Mr. Goodby, along with an explanatory note.

Goodby, Silverstein & Partners

December 16, 1997

Naomi Shavin
980 Edgewater Drive NW
Atlanta, Georgia 30328

Dear Naomi:

Thanks so much for your nice letter about our
"got milk" commercials. I particularly liked
the fact that you were having a baked potato
with your milk. This is very unusual.

Adding things to milk to make it taste better is
a really good idea. For my children, I put
milk, peanut butter, a banana, and a little
maple syrup in a blender. They drink this
almost every morning.

You are a really good artist. I especially liked
the way you drew your dress.

Thanks for your note. We'll keep your picture
on our wall.

Yours,

Jeff Goodby
Creative Director

Dear Mr. Goodby,

   Thank you for the wonderful things. I'm going to use my T-shirt and my "Got Milk?" glass today. I loved the bubble paper best.

Love and milk,

Naomi

Dear Evander,

My brother has a bully in his class. What should he do? He thinks he should punch him and hit him and kick him and throw him into the mud. I told him he should say, "Stop it or I'll tell the teacher. It's not nice and it's bothering me."

How big are your muscles? Adam is 3.

Once we were playing under our Grandpa's chair and it almost fell on us. I told Adam to go away while I fixed the chair and that's how I saved Adam.

Love and punches,

Naomi

Naomi is very protective of her younger brother, which is a nice way of saying no one can torment him but her.

130

Holyfield
M A N A G E M E N T

EVANDER HOLYFIELD
THREE TIME HEAVYWEIGHT
CHAMPION OF THE WORLD
CHAIRMAN

Dr. Janice M. Holyfield
Chief Executive Officer

February 6, 1998

Naomi Shavin
980 Edgewater Dr. N.W.
Atlanta, Ga 30328
Fulton

Dear ,

Thank you for your inquiry regarding Mr. Evander Holyfield. We greatly appreciate your kind and complimentary remarks. We apologize for the delay in response to your letter requesting an autograph from Mr. Holyfield.

Due to the large volume of correspondence received, Mr. Holyfield is unable to respond personally to everyone. However he would like to encourage you to respect your parent, study hard in school and remember Phillipians 4:13.

Enclosed, please find two pictures of Mr. Holyfield. We sincerely hope it comes at a convenient time for your project.

Again, thank you for your interest in the WBA Heavyweight Champion of the World Evander Holyfield.

Best Regards,

Gilda Byrd
Office Assistant

794 HWY 279 ◆ FAIRBURN, GA 30213
PHONE (770) 460-6807 ◆ FAX (770) 460-5381

Dear Rabbi Goodman,

    I am glad that you like my drawings.

    When were the dinosaurs made? Were they made before or after the flood?

    God made a masterpiece and at night it came alive. There were two people who were getting engaged. God took the world and rolled it into a ball. The people had children and they had children and they had children.

Love,

Naomi

RABBI ARNOLD M. GOODMAN

AHAVATH ACHIM SYNAGOGUE
600 PEACHTREE BATTLE AVENUE, N.E.
ATLANTA • GEORGIA 30327
404-355-5222

February 10, 1998
14 Shevat 5758

Dear Naomi,

You ask very good questions, and they are not always easy to answer. When did God make the dinosaurs? All animals were created before the flood. The question is since dinosaurs were so big, how did Noah fit them into the ark? I really don't know the answer to that question but maybe he had a hole in the ceiling so the dinosaurs' heads would stick out. If there was a hole in the ceiling, everyone would have gotten wet. Maybe the dinosaurs had an umbrella over their heads.

God rolled the earth into a ball so that it could spin around the sun making morning and night, as well as seasons of the year. After God made all the animals, He made Adam and Eve. Some people think He made Eve out of the rib of Adam. Others think that Adam and Eve were created at the same time and in the same way. The Bible leads us to believe that either theory may be correct. What's important is that after God created Adam and Eve, He wanted them to become engaged, get married and have children. In fact having children was the first commandment He gave them, and whenever a mommy and daddy have a baby, they are doing exactly what God wants them to do.

I know your mommy and daddy are very happy that you were born, and then Adam, and now Sarah. This Shabbat, all of you will be at Synagogue, and we will say a special prayer to celebrate Sarah's birth who is very lucky to have a big sister like you and a big brother like Adam.

If you have any more questions, please write to me, and I will be happy to try and answer them.

Your friend,

RABBI ARNOLD M. GOODMAN

Dear Rabbi Goodman,

Why did Hashem make Hitler if he was going to kill the Jews? In school I learned about Hitler and that is why I am writing to you.

Who or what made Hashem? How did Hashem make people be able to move around? Why do people die?

Love,

Naomi

P.S. I am sorry this is messy.

A child's questions can be direct and yet deal with complicated themes that are among the most difficult to address. We were driving home from a beach vacation, tanned and rested, when Naomi—out the blue—snapped us back to reality with a question about Hashem (God) and the Holocaust. Her mother and I looked at each other, momentarily speechless, then drove for many miles contemplating aloud the question that Naomi raises in her third letter to her rabbi.

RABBI ARNOLD M. GOODMAN

AHAVATH ACHIM SYNAGOGUE
600 PEACHTREE BATTLE AVENUE, N.E.
ATLANTA • GEORGIA 30327
404-355-5222

July 22, 1998
28 Tammuz 5758

Dear Naomi,

You ask very good questions which are not always easy to answer.

Why did God or Hashem make Hitler who was a very bad man? God made the first two people, Adam and Eve. From then on people make babies who are raised by their parents and families. God also told Adam and Eve that they and all other people would have to make their own choices as to how they would behave. We call this free will. Most people decide to do good things in their lives. It's very sad that there always some people who do bad things. Hitler did very bad things especially to the Jews. God did punish him, but it took a long time and lots of people were killed by him. I don't believe God was happy with this, but He would never take away our ability to decide what kind of life we want to live.

Who made Hashem? That's a question for which there is no answer. We call such questions—mysteries. God just has always been, and there was never a time when He didn't exist. It's hard to imagine that God has always been, but that why it's a mystery.

How did God make people move about? God made us with legs to be able to move from place to place. He just figured out that if we didn't have legs and had to move around on our bellies we would be like snakes, and He didn't think that people should be like snakes and have to crawl on their bellies and live on the ground. It sure is more convenient and lot more comfortable being able to walk, to run, to hop and to skip which we could never do if we didn't have legs. So God did a great thing when he designed us the way He did.

Why do people die? This world can only accommodate so many people. If no one ever died then there would soon be no room for new people and people would stop having babies and that would be a great loss since babies are fun to have around. So God decided that every person would be born and begin living. Being alive is like being on a trip - a nice trip - with your mommy and daddy and Adam and Sarah and your grandparents. At different stops God may ask someone to leave the trip, and to join Him in heaven. We then go on without them. If God is good to us we have a long and wonderful trip with lots of singing and dancing and fun and vacations and the people we love keep on traveling with us.

I hope these answers aren't too long for you. It's fun for me to try to answer your questions.

Finally thanks for the drawings you sent me. They are very nice.

Please say hello to your mother and father and to Adam and Sarah for me.

Sincerely yours,

RABBI ARNOLD M. GOODMAN

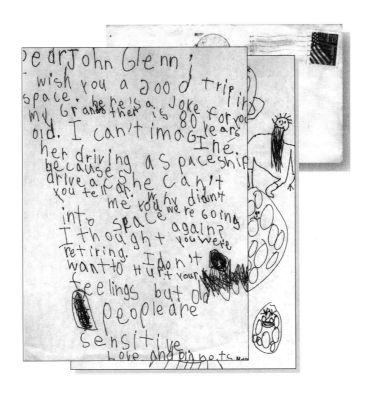

Dear John Glenn,

I wish you a good trip in space.

Here's a joke for you. My grandmother is 80 years old. I can't imagine her driving a spaceship because she can't drive a car.

Why didn't you tell me you were going into space again? I thought you were retiring. I don't want to hurt your feelings, but old people are sensitive.

Love and planets,

Naomi

One minute he's announcing his retirement from the Senate, and the next he's resuming his career as an astronaut.

United States Senate

WASHINGTON, DC 20510–3501

March 22, 1998

Naomi Shavin
980 Edgewater Drive
Atlanta, GA 30328

Dear Naomi:

Thank you for your letter asking about my participation in the space program. I hope this letter and materials I am enclosing will answer most of your questions.

When I was growing up no one took space travel seriously. We dreamt of flying airplanes and exploring far away places on earth, but adventures in space were only talked about in fantasy and fiction - in fact the word astronaut did not even exist.

I was excited when I learned I was to be one of the first people in space. Many people have asked me if I was scared, but I looked forward to learning new things and going someplace no one had ever been before.

The name of my spaceship was Friendship 7, and it actually was very tiny. I stayed strapped into my seat most of the time because of the weightlessness. Weightlessness allows everything to float because there is no gravity to hold anything down. All food was kept in containers like toothpaste tubes so I could squeeze them directly into my mouth - food on a plate would have begun floating around the cabin.

It was very exciting to look out from space and see planet earth. It was like a round ball floating in the air, and I could see the rivers, road, and cities, just like on pictures you have probably seen taken from space.

Maybe someday you can even go into space, perhaps explore farther than I did. As long as you continue to study and work hard you can achieve anything.

Best regards.

Sincerely,

John Glenn
United States Senator

JG/kco

Dear Satellite Company,

This is the way you can get the satellite in the right orbit. You get a team and send them up to outer space. Then they bring a big lasso and they lasso the satellite and put the satellite in the right orbit. Then the beepers will work.

How do you make satellites?

Love,

Naomi

At the breakfast table one morning, I showed Naomi a newspaper illustration of the troubled Galaxy IV satellite, the one that caused all the pager problems. She interrupted me to say, "I know all about that." It seems that the McNeil-Lehrer News Hour comes on after Barney, and if the stories are interesting, she watches. Not only did she watch the story about the errant satellite, she knew how to fix it.

May 29, 1998

Miss Naomi Shavin
980 Edgewater Drive NW
Atlanta, Georgia 30328

Dear Naomi,

Thank you for sending us your wonderful idea on how to get our satellite in the right orbit.

All of our engineers and scientists thought you came up with a good idea. They are going to talk about your idea at a big meeting and I am sure the other people there will think it is a great idea too. Everyone especially liked your drawing with the moon and the stars.

We are happy to tell you that all the beepers are working. We are going to send more satellites into space this year, so maybe you will see another TV show about PanAmSat satellites.

It is very hard to make a satellite. First, very smart people sit around a table and make drawings of how it should look. Then they send their drawings to some other people who work in a big factory. The people at the factory make parts and when they are done, everyone gets together and puts the parts together to make a satellite. You can find pictures about this in the book we are sending you.

We all hope you will like the hat, shirt and frisbee.

Thank you, again.

Sincerely,

Ursela Krackow
PanAmSat

140

Dear Orange Growers,

I love oranges. The only thing I don't like is the seeds. Then they invented seedless oranges. I like the seedless oranges better. How do you grow seedless oranges when there aren't any seeds?

Your orange-eater,

Naomi

Sunkist®

April 9, 1998

Sunkist Growers
Post Office Box 7888
Van Nuys, CA 91409-7888
Tel: (818) 986-4800

Miss Naomi Shavin
980 Edgewater Drive NW
Atlanta, GA 30328

Dear Naomi:

Thank you so much for your nice letter and picture, wanting to know how we grow seedless navel oranges without having seeds to start with.

Well, it's sort of difficult to explain but I'll try. You need to think of a seedless navel orange tree as "two trees in one." First, the nurserymen plant a seed from a tree that produces oranges with seeds. Then when the seed turns into a young seedling (about a year old), they take a bud from a pre-existing navel orange tree and graft the bud onto the young tree. So, when the tree grows up, its roots and part of its trunk are one type of tree, but the top of the tree (where the fruit is grown) is a different type of tree, and one which produces seedless oranges.

I hope I've explained it in a way that you can understand. Thank you for taking the time to write us with such a good question.

Sincerely,

Patti Dunlap

Patti Dunlap
Manager
Consumer Response Center

PPD:ccb

Dear Marcus Pfister,

How do you make the glittery stuff on your books? I like your books. My class was reading *Milo and the Magic Stone*. Love,
Naomi

The Rainbow Fish, *by Marcus Pfister, is one of Naomi's favorite books. In it, a beautiful fish, consumed by pride, learns the value of sharing. At school, Naomi read another Pfister book,* Milo and the Magic Stone. *The shimmering illustrations are a hallmark of Pfister's books, and they sparked a discussion among Naomi's classmates. Because she writes letters, Naomi was appointed to find out how he works his magic. Not only did Pfister write back, he drew Naomi a picture.*

For Naomi!

Dear Naomi

Thank you very much for your letter and
your cover illustrations of my books - they
just look great! I'm happy that you enjoyed
my storys. The glittering parts in the books are
stamped after the normal print of the books
into them. I only have to mask where the
glittering scales and stones have to be.
I wish you a nice summer.   Your friend

Dear Mom and Dad,

I love you more than the planet loves its beauty.

I love you more than the sun loves its shine.

I love you more than the moon loves its glow.

I love you more than the lightning bug loves its light.

Love,

Naomi

Naomi's letters have been, by turns, tender and silly, serious and sad. They have taught Naomi about a wealth of subjects, even stimulated her interest in history, geography, and stamps. They have made her feel she has a voice in the world—a voice that is heard and respected in the halls of academe and the halls of Congress, in a tiny, isolated village in Alaska and in Buckingham Palace. But more than anything else these letters represent time spent together, talking about the world, talking to each other, finding in pen and ink a companionship that knows no boundaries.